healing with gems and crystals

Kristyna Arcati

GW00497291

With grateful thanks to Paul for his help

Hodder Education

Hodder Education is an Hachette UK company
First published in UK 2011 by Hodder Education.
Copyright © 2011 Kristyna Arcati
The moral rights of the author have been asserted.
Database right Hodder Education (makers).

All rights reserved. No part of this publication may be reproduced, stored in
a retrieval system or transmitted in any form or by any means, electronic,
mechanical, photocopying, recording or otherwise, without the prior
permission in writing of Hodder Education, or as expressly permitted by law,
or under terms agreed with the appropriate reprographic rights organization.
Enquiries concerning reproduction outside the scope of the above should be
sent to the Rights Department, Hodder Education

You must not circulate this book in any other binding or cover and you must
impose this same condition on any acquirer.

British Library Cataloguing in Publication Data: a catalogue record for this title
is available from the British Library.

10 9 8 7 6 5 4 3 2 1

The publisher has used its best endeavours to ensure that any website
addresses referred to in this book are correct and active at the time of going
to press. However, the publisher and the author have no responsibility for the
websites and can make no guarantee that a site will remain live or that the
content will remain relevant, decent or appropriate.

The publisher has made every effort to mark as such all words which it
believes to be trademarks. The publisher should also like to make it clear that
the presence of a word in the book, whether marked or unmarked, in no way
affects its legal status as a trademark.

Every reasonable effort has been made by the publisher to trace the copyright
holders of material in this book. Any errors or omissions should be notified in
writing to the publisher, who will endeavour to rectify the situation for any
reprints and future editions.

Hachette UK's policy is to use papers that are natural, renewable and
recyclable products and made from wood grown in sustainable forests.
The logging and manufacturing processes are expected to conform to the
environmental regulations of the country of origin.

Typeset by MPS Limited, a Macmillan Company.

Contents

1

making a start

Thinking of crystals and gemstones, do you picture little stones set in jewellery or chunks (more properly, 'clusters') of coloured rock of varying sizes? The raw natural state, or cut stone, polished and sparkling? This book will discuss all sorts of crystals and gemstones, look at their many uses and explore their potential as aids in our development.

People start to collect or buy crystals and gemstones for various reasons – perhaps as ornaments or as an investment. For some, crystals and gemstones are a key to learning.

What are your reasons? Do you wish to contact your higher self? Use a stone for healing? Do you like the colour and texture of the stones? Do you choose stones to match your zodiac sign? Is your interest in dowsing? Do you wish to use a crystal in a pendulum? Or rid your aura of negativities? In every case, learning more about the crystal or gemstone will help you use it to its full potential.

This first chapter explains how to choose a crystal or stone and prepare it for its work.

I have been in a shop selling crystals and gemstones and felt compelled, for a reason I cannot explain, to buy a certain stone. When this happens I always buy the stone; I know that the reason will eventually become apparent. I keep the stone in a safe place ready for its use in the future. Often a stone has come into its own months after my purchase of it. I have also heard it said that you should pick up a lot of crystals at the same time; whichever stone seems to 'stick' to your fingers is the one for you.

However, when deciding whether to buy a stone, look at it carefully, even if it is begging you to buy it. Chipped or broken stones may have reduced energies and so be unable to help in specific healing situations. Each stone has its own energy field, or 'piezoelectricity'. This means that there are vibrations in and around each stone. It is what gives the stones power – energy is the source of power. Anything that lessens the energy (such as a chip) reduces the efficacy of the stone.

Be sure to handle the stone or crystal you intend to buy. Some people who are sensitive to energy vibrations may feel a tingling sensation with some stones, and nothing with others. Professional crystal therapists argue that a tingling sensation from a crystal is a sign of negativity and that the stone should, therefore, not be purchased, as it is not meant to be used. The thing to remember is that you must feel right with the stone – and in order to fully connect with the stone, you may find it useful to mentally ask the stone if it is right for you, or the person for whom it is intended, and see whether you get any impression one way or the other.

Each crystal and gemstone is unique and one may not feel the same as another. People working in shops selling crystals and gemstones are used to their customers spending time choosing stones and will expect you to look at and handle many stones before you single one out. Pick up each stone in turn. If you feel happy with one, put it to one side but make sure you touch others before making a firm decision. Try the stones in both hands, not just the hand you normally use. Move them around in your hands, look at them from every angle, and buy the stone you feel happiest with.

We shall now look briefly at crystals and gemstones separately.

Choosing your crystal

If you are thinking of purchasing only crystals, remember that they are forms of quartz, formed naturally over centuries, and usually imported, so they could be expensive. Quartz crystals come in many colours and have various names. Pure quartz crystal is clear-coloured, but amethyst is also a quartz, as are stones such as rose quartz, milky quartz and smoky quartz. Quartz is a very common, powerful mineral, which has a strong link with the human race and with consciousness in particular. Crystals can come in clusters or in clear points, one end pointed and the other end not. Pure quartz crystals have six faces, but imperfections may slightly alter the structure.

The price of crystals varies enormously, depending on their quality and size. The factor that should guide your purchase is the clarity of the stone, not the size or shape, or even the price. When you find a crystal, look carefully into its centre and satisfy yourself that there are as few imperfections as possible. If you are considering using the crystal for healing, think about the shape a little more. Some people using crystals for healing prefer one end to be either pointed or rounded. If you are thinking of using the crystal to enhance dreams, the shape may not be so important. If you are looking for a crystal to charge other stones or to create energy in a room, you may need to think about a larger cluster, as a larger crystal will have a larger energy field around it. Rose quartz may be the crystal to use for this sort of work. An uncut crystal is always more powerful than one that has been cut.

Choosing your gemstone

Like crystals, gemstones come in a variety of shapes, sizes and prices. Some gemstones are more difficult to excavate or to locate in the first place and so may be expensive, for example Lapis lazuli. While price may not necessarily be the main factor in your choice, make sure that you are happy with what you are getting. As with crystals, look to see if the stone is chipped, imperfect or impaired in any way before making a final decision to buy.

Choosing a supplier

There are a number of specialist mineral agents who deal in crystals and gemstones. Many advertise in national papers as well as magazines covering New Age issues. Some agents offer a postal service only. Personally, I always prefer to go to a shop selling crystals and gemstones and look around. There may be several in your area and I would advise you to look at all the possible suppliers to ascertain the quality, as well as the price, before embarking on a definite shopping expedition.

Some stones, such as smoky quartz and citrine, can be man-made. The colours of man-made stones will not be true, and it is important to talk to the supplier and, if possible, find out the country of origin of the stone, so you know it is what it is claimed to be. Once you become used to handling stones, you will develop a feel for the genuine article.

Cleansing your stone

Now you have your crystal or gemstone, you should be aware that many people have handled it, and it should be cleansed of any negativities it may have picked up from human contact or the environment in which it was kept. You also need to clean it in the generally accepted sense. Some maintain that the stone will have within it the memory of having been plucked from the earth and the pain associated with that excavation. Others may disagree, but whatever you think, you need to cleanse, charge and programme your new acquisition. Bypassing this necessary stage can prevent the crystal or gemstone from acting in the way you intend. Also, using a crystal or gemstone that is not properly cleansed of its negativities can lead to headaches. It is important to note that beginners may find themselves subject to headaches if in close contact with large crystal clusters, as the power from these is very strong. So, if you intend to use a large crystal cluster, make sure it is never kept in the bedroom, as it could cause you problems. The process of cleansing your stone is not difficult and will help you to bond with it.

Cleansing with water

There are several ways to cleanse crystals and gemstones. One is water purification – holding them under clear, running water, preferably in a natural setting. I always take my crystals to a nearby stream to cleanse them. Other people may prefer to use mineral water (not tap water) or sea water. One thing to remember about mineral water is that it may be irradiated, in which case don't use it.

It is important to focus your thoughts on clearing the stone of its impurities. Some people always say the same few words. Others say nothing but focus their attention on purity and a white or gold light. Do whatever you feel comfortable with.

If you are using bottled water, it is probably best to leave the stone in the water overnight. As the water is not running, extra time is needed. Some people like to leave their stone in the water in direct sunlight. Others, who may have a connection with the moon, leave the stone in the water in the moonlight. It is said that the sun will help to energise, while the moon will cleanse. Generally, I consider that the best time for cleansing a crystal with moonlight is during the waning of the moon, i.e. in its last quarter. Others suggest the best time is during the first quarter, when the moon is waxing.

Cleansing with earth

For this method of cleansing, you can bury your crystal overnight in the garden; or, if you have no garden or earth in which to bury your stone, use salt, preferably sea or rock salt. Again, as you bury the stone, you need to focus on the reasons for cleansing it. Cleansing with earth may take more time than cleansing with water, and some authorities claim it is necessary to leave the stone covered in earth, or salt, for several days. Three days seems to be a generally agreed length of time. If you use salt, make sure that you discard it afterwards, as it soaks up negativities which may then be transferred to a future stone. If you bury the crystal outside, try to use an area of garden that is not cultivated and has not been polluted with pesticides or treated with fertilisers.

Cleansing with air

You may like to try cleansing your stone with air. There are several ways of doing this. If you feel you can offer the stone meditational breathing, you may sit with it, focusing your attention on the stone, and consciously breathe white light on the stone.

Cleansing with fire

Using a candle or natural flame, sit in meditation with your stone and visualise the flame from the candle or fire cleansing the stone of its impurities. When you have done this, swiftly pass the stone through the flame, taking care not to burn yourself or harm the crystal in any way. This process can lead to a sooty deposit around the outside of your stone. Gently wash this off in running water and the stone will be cleansed.

How often to cleanse

Crystals that are used often or carried around regularly will need regular cleansing. Some people suggest once a week.

It is important to realise that crystals soak up the atmosphere in which they are kept. If kept in a room where stress or tension levels often run high, the stones will absorb this negativity and possibly need more frequent cleansing. Likewise, if a major argument occurs in a room where the crystals or gemstones are kept, it is vital to cleanse them as soon as the tensions lift, especially if you yourself have been involved in the difficulties. If you use stones for healing, always cleanse them after a healing session, as they pick up negativities from the patient.

How long to cleanse

It is worth noting that dark crystals take more cleansing than others because the energies they hold go deep. Therefore you should take more time cleansing dark stones, such as obsidian. It is also necessary to cleanse diamonds for a long time, because they are a very hard stone. Man-made stones also need longer cleansing times, and zircon in particular falls into this category.

Charging your stone

Having cleansed and cleaned your crystal or gemstone, you must charge it with the positive energies it will need to work effectively for you.

Again, there are several ways of doing this. Some people like to leave their stone in the moonlight or sunlight (either outside or in the house) for a few days. Others prefer to wait for thunderstorms or very hot or very cold spells. Some people place their cleansed crystal with a programmer or generator crystal (usually a large crystal or amethyst cluster which will send out its own energies). Others place their crystals and gemstones within a pyramid. The programmer crystal I have is huge: it is a chunk of quartz weighing three and a half pounds, with over 80 separate crystal points, some large and some very small. It looks like a plain with a mountain rising from its middle and is a truly beautiful object.

The easiest way to charge your new acquisition is to sit with it in quiet and solitude and focus your attention on it in detail. If you are happy meditating, go into a brief meditation with the stone and envisage a white light enveloping both you and your stone.

Alternatively, imagine yourself going through a door within the crystal and becoming one with the stone. Imagine yourself feeling the structure of the stone and its surfaces. This process is generally best held for at least five minutes.

Some people who are unaccustomed to meditation feel quite happy charging their stones by holding them close to their heart and picturing a calm scene – woodland or something similar. Focusing the attention on the reason for the purchase of the gemstone or crystal will also charge the stone effectively.

Programming your stone

Once it is clean, cleansed and charged, you need to programme the crystal or gemstone for the work it is expected to do. This is probably the most vital part of preparing a stone and you must be sure of the work you intend for it. Healing crystals must be programmed to work within a healing framework. If you are using your stone for meditation, it must be programmed to work this way. However, if you don't yet have a specific task for the stone, keep it in a bag or pouch, wrapped in a natural fabric, until you decide what use you intend for it. Some authorities suggest that you should carry the stone around with you for a month so that you bond with the crystal, if you are not programming it. Again, do what you feel is right for you and the stone in question.

Programming the crystal involves finding a quiet place and a few minutes to relax. Place the stone between your eyebrows in the place known as the 'third eye' at the 'brow chakra', and concentrate on linking with the crystal, all the time thinking of the work you intend the stone to do for you.

It is important to dedicate the use of the crystal or gemstone for good only. This is an irreversible part of the programming. If you even attempt to programme for evil, the stone will not accept your negative energies. If you decide to change the use of your stone, you will need to reprogramme it.

Where to keep your stone

Ideally, you should keep the stone near direct sunlight. Tradition suggests that people intending to use their stone for meditation or inspirational purposes should keep their stone in moonlight for several days before using it. Whatever you do, make sure that your stone sees natural light. A product of nature and of the earth, it needs natural light as much as you do.

If you have a large piece of crystal that you use for generating or programming, keep your new acquisition near to this. I keep my huge piece of crystal in the centre of all my other stones. This keeps them all charged and ready for use.

As with other tools of self-enlightenment, treat your crystals and gemstones with respect. Don't let anyone play with them – they are not toys. If you feel happy talking to them, by all means do so. I admit to talking to both my crystals and my plants! Show them love and consideration and they will respond.

Special types of stone

Control crystals

Control crystals are sometimes also called 'generator crystals' and should ideally be single-terminated quartz – that is one that comes to one single point. It may take a long time before the right quartz makes itself known to you. The more involved you become in crystal healing, the sooner you may find your generator crystal.

These quartz crystals can re-energise other crystals. They can help to cleanse rooms of negativities, and are also used to cleanse the body. For this, they are held in the hand and moved in a spiral from top to bottom of the body and back up again.

Jewellery

It is just as important to cleanse jewellery as it is to cleanse your newly acquired crystals and gemstones. Items of jewellery, especially rings, are with you almost all the time. They pick up negativities and need regular cleansing, in the same way as stones that stay inside your home.

The joints of the body can store negativities, which may account for the large number of people with arthritis and other joint problems, and so rings, especially those with dark stones, need cleansing very often. Not doing so can lead to rheumatic problems for the wearer. Cleansing jewellery by moonlight is probably the most effective method.

Metal is said by many authorities to inhibit healing energies, so if you are intending to buy a stone and wear it for healing purposes, or to use a stone in dowsing or as a pendulum, make sure that it has a non-metallic clasp (if worn as a necklace). If possible, it should have no contact with metal at all. The best way of wearing a stone is around the neck on a thong. It is also worth noting that spherical shapes are better for healing than rough or tumbled stones.

Crystal energy rods

These rods, often quite simple structures, have been used throughout history to help tap into energy fields. They should not be confused with 'magic wands', although they do also appear in fairy tales.

Copper is the most conductive of the crystalline forms, as it channels all forms of energy. This explains why copper bracelets are useful for rheumatic conditions. Crystal will help collect and amplify this 'anatonic energy' (also sometimes called 'primal energy').

Copper rods need to be capped at the end you intend to hold, as this allows interchange between the rod and the bio-plasmic energy of the body. Standard copper pipe is often used and 30 centimetres (12 inches) is the usual length.

Place the crystal at one end, avoiding the use of glue and having pre-programmed your crystal to work with the rod. The crystal used must be clear quartz. Keep the copper pipe free from obstructions to allow the energy to spiral down the pipe.

Using the rod can help clear rooms of negative energies. Other gemstones can also interact with the rod, especially amethyst, but must be placed at the 'cap' end. It is important to leave the copper surface showing at the quartz end a little, in order to draw in the anatonic energy.

If using a rod, make sure you feel comfortable with it and relaxed. If you intend to try using such a rod for healing other people, make sure they feel happy about it, as some people feel very uncomfortable with rods.

Absent healing stones

Using a crystal or gemstone for absent healing is a very common practice. The effects of this healing can go worldwide.

If you are thinking of buying a stone for such a purpose, it is best to think in terms of a clear, single-terminated piece of quartz crystal, with the point upright. Amethyst can be used, as can fluorite; both are carriers of a particularly strong type of energy, known as 'purple ray' energy.

Stones for absent healing must be programmed for only this function. When in use, they should be clasped with both hands, and they should be stored in contact with untreated wood or earth.

We will be discussing healing in the next chapter, but for absent healing, all that is necessary is to obtain a 'signature', that is, something belonging to the person for whom the healing is intended (hair, letter, photo, for example). Place your stone by this 'signature'. Ask the crystal for help for this person, not for a cure, but for retardation of illness or for general healing aid.

Using this process you can ask for absent healing for any number of people, in any number of places or countries, as long as each has an individual 'signature'. Once the person has recovered, or no longer needs absent healing, you can remove the 'signature', making sure you thank the crystal for its help in the process.

Crystal balls

Nowadays, most crystal balls are not actually crystal but glass, because crystal is so expensive. A crystal ball acts as a focus in meditational work or as an aid to developing intuition. Pictures are seen inside the globe. Some people maintain that these come from the subconscious, while others suggest a more mystic source. All the crystal ball does is help the user to focus on the work in hand, to enter into a meditative state and open themselves up to images.

Traditionally, a crystal ball should be a gift and not purchased by the person intending to use it. The person who gave me mine was not a crystal reader but she did have a crystal ball and gave it to me when she realised I could use it in my work.

A true crystal ball is likely to be very expensive. You will need to cleanse, clean, charge and programme it in exactly the same way as for crystals and gemstones, and also to polish it, preferably with a chamois leather, before leaving it in the sunlight for a few hours. After this process, nobody should touch the globe, other than yourself. People coming to you wishing to receive direction from the crystal ball must not touch it. They may hold their hands above it, by all means, but never touch it. They must not look into it either.

2

power
behind
the stones

One major use for crystals is in healing – for yourself, another or in 'absent healing'.

Healing is not the same as curing. It helps the body, or mind, to become stronger and consequently better. It involves looking at the person as an entity, not at separate symptoms. Curing restores physical health, with symptoms being treated. It is the job of qualified doctors. Always see a doctor about health problems. Healing with crystals complements, but does not replace, medical care.

To live life to its full potential, we need good health. Sometimes we fall foul of disease or illness. If you think of 'dis-ease' as being ill at ease with yourself, you are half-way to understanding the bridge between body and mind. Crystals and gemstones can help repair a broken link in that bridge, allowing the body's own healing processes to work as intended. Often, ill health occurs because of the stresses and strains of daily life... We let outside situations cause us problems. Learning there are ways to help ourselves overcome the problems can lead to better health.

Over the ages, many civilisations have practised healing with crystals and gemstones. People in ancient Egypt, Tibet, India and China all used stones for healing, as did (and in some cases still do) some American Indian tribes, Australian Aboriginals and African tribes.

It is important to understand that, in carrying out crystal healing, we ourselves are not doing the healing. We are merely helping to alleviate blockages, so that the body can heal itself. Therefore, never claim you are a healer. You are simply helping the healing process. Even fully qualified crystal therapists never claim to be able to cure a problem. If they do, they are not sound practitioners. Most importantly, the information I give in this book is not sufficient for you to start healing others professionally. All I hope to do is show you the various ways in which crystals and gemstones can be used and perhaps spark an interest that will stimulate you to undertake further training.

When thinking of healing, you need to think about the physical body, the spiritual body and the aura and chakras. Later we will discuss healing the seven chakra centres specifically, but you need to appreciate from the outset that they are the body's own energy centres, and correspond with the seven colours and the seven planets. You also need to realise that your dreams may be messages from your subconscious concerning healing that the body requires.

Do you need to be psychic to heal?

This is a common question and the answer is that you don't, but – and this is a big but – you have to be sensitive to other people and their needs, anxieties and concerns. You must also genuinely want to help and feel able to link with your patient, with only the best intent. There are no hard-and-fast rules about healing with crystals, but various methods can be adopted and we will discuss some of these as we progress.

A main requirement for being a good healer is the ability to raise the energy level of the patient. Energy rises, and it is necessary to raise energies from the bottom (the feet) to the top (the crown of the head). Many healers forget this, leave their patient's energy permanently 'grounded' and then wonder why the healing energies are not working properly. Remember too that you may find yourself subject to what are known as 'pranic energies' (numbness or tingling in your hands when carrying out healing). Make sure you shake your hands and wash them in cold water. Failure to do this can give you arthritic problems in the future.

Bear in mind that you are a beginner and untrained. We will discuss methods of healing and how to start healing, but you must accept, and always make it clear to friends you endeavour to help through healing with crystals and gemstones, that you are not properly trained, and will not know all the answers.

The question of diagnosis

Unless you are medically qualified, even if you become a trained crystal therapist, *never diagnose*. It is not your job to do so. You should always encourage your patient to visit their GP or medical practitioner and make it clear that any medication prescribed *must* be taken as directed. People may think they know what is wrong with themselves or with others, but unless they are medically qualified or have received a medical diagnosis, they can be very wide of the mark. It is not unknown for the body to produce symptoms as a result of worry or stress which, to the untrained eye, could be taken as symptoms of a condition totally unrelated to the real problem. Remember that you are there to try to help, not create more anxieties than are already present.

Healing crystals and gemstones

As explained in Chapter 1, a stone used for healing must be kept for that purpose alone. Stones for healing are special and must be kept clean and cared for. Consider keeping them wrapped in a natural fabric or in paper. However, don't forget that they will still need to see regular sunlight to function properly. It is not necessary to choose only one stone for a specific problem. Remember to think of all the possible stones that could help.

If you are intending to use a personal healing stone, it can be kept round your neck on a thong, but remember: *no metal*. Some therapists will disagree but I feel confident that it is better to avoid metal wherever possible in connection with crystals and gemstones.

Also remember that you must cleanse your stones regularly so they don't become blocked with negativities accumulated from people's ill health. It is best to cleanse and clean every time you heal with a stone.

Selecting a room for healing

Make sure you use an appropriate room for healing. People skilled in the use of pendulums, or those who have made themselves a pendulum from a crystal intending to use it for healing (see Chapter 3), may like to use it to search for the most appropriate room for healing by dowsing over a sketch plan of the house. Suggest to the crystal that it looks for specific positive and negative energies in that room.

Look at the room from the outsider's viewpoint. Colours are very important – they must blend and soothe. Many healing rooms are blue, as blue light in a healing room helps the client open up and discuss problems. Green is also good for aiding the flow of healing energy. Any patterns in wallpaper must be flowing and wavy, rather than straight or pointed. As the ceiling relates to the crown chakra (the top of the head), it should preferably be white, tinted with either blue or pink.

Make sure that the floor is clean and uncluttered. Dark flooring creates a good atmosphere; patterned carpets can cause problems. Curtains should be thick enough to shut out the light, and blinds are often good for this purpose.

Lighting should be soft but it shouldn't be too dark. Spotlights, if reflecting into corners, are acceptable, but make sure the lighting is soft. Never have a light facing the door, as the person entering will see the light before anything else.

Chairs should be comfortable and not too low for people with mobility problems. People often bring friends along for moral support, so have extra chairs available, but make sure any friends sit out of the way in a corner, if possible.

The crystals you are intending to use should be kept together and be easily visible, on a trolley or table, and near to the person requiring therapy.

If you have access to a couch, use it by all means. Some people use beds, and if you are intending to do this, make sure the mattress is soft and made of natural fibres; and, again, think about the colour.

You will need water, both for you and the patient. You may also need a bowl to wash your hands and a towel to dry them.

Think about a blanket for the patient. Offer it; don't force it on the person.

Creating the right atmosphere

Always allow the person to talk about his or her problems. Make sure you listen. Don't ask what the problem is, just listen. Make them feel wanted and show that you are interested in what they are saying. People often like to be touched or greeted warmly when they come for healing. If you are sure the person will not recoil from it, give them a hug and create some warmth and contact. Try to use first names and indulge in a little small talk to help them unwind. The chances are they will be very nervous (you may be nervous yourself) and a little chat about themselves, leading on to a few words about crystals, will help you both to relax.

Say just a few words about the stones and what you will try to do. Don't bore the person with technical information about crystals and their properties and uses. Using complicated words can create barriers and we need to break down barriers, not create them. Background music can be helpful. Make sure you have eye contact with the person, as it helps to forge a link.

If you intend to use different stones for the healing session, show these to the person. Ask them to sit without crossing their legs or arms, and position your seat slightly to one side of them. Never turn your back on the person, even when you go to fetch your tray of stones. If you think a particular stone is appropriate for the healing, show it to the person.

If you and the person coming for therapy feel happy with crystal meditation, this is a good way of bringing about strong healing. However, it is important to talk this through first.

After the healing session

After a healing session, suggest that the person stretches out. The healing energies will stay with them after the session and you should warn them about this and explain that if they feel very tired later, they must sit or lie down, and relax, because this is a signal that the healing is repeating itself. It is important that they understand this process. Get them to ask any questions before they leave, before the link is broken.

Very rarely, a person will feel worse after a session. Sometimes the person accompanying them and not taking part in the healing itself may also feel rather unwell. Explain that there is still negative energy to be removed, and supply a healing crystal (such as tourmaline) or a gem elixir (discussed later on) to help. Rest should be recommended.

Natural signs of problems

You may be able to take one look at a person and have a rough idea what the problem is, especially if it relates to mobility. However, as we have said, try not to diagnose, even mentally to yourself.

Make sure you also look for 'hidden emotions'. People who are tense or nervous, who avoid physical contact, sit with crossed arms or legs, have a tight smile on their lips, or fidget are usually people with emotional or nervous problems. Try to get such people to talk freely, rather than just giving 'Yes/No' answers. Don't ask too many questions, but encourage them to start thinking about the crystals in a gentle, unforced way. Ask them to handle a few stones.

If they feel warmth in their hands at this stage, it is an indication of healing, and so saying something such as 'When you find the warmth coming, you will start to feel more relaxed and at ease' will help the relaxation process and aid in the healing.

People who are angry are difficult to work with because they often have low self-esteem. Angry people tend to give short, sharp answers and appear to bite back rather than reply naturally. They also avoid eye contact. Pyrite is very effective for such people, as we will discuss later. People who are hyperactive can be helped with crystals, in particular with smoky quartz and haematite.

People showing such signs of negativity can have an effect on you personally. Try not to let this happen, as the healing process can be impaired by your own negativities joining forces with theirs.

You may occasionally come across someone who is dependent on drugs or alcohol, or seriously ill. These people should be directed towards a professional crystal therapist, as the work required to help them is intense. It would also be prudent to suggest that they might like other professional help and/or guidance. However, they must seek this help of their own volition.

Healing with a crystal rod

Once you have made sure that the person feels happy with your using a crystal rod, ask them to stand with their legs slightly apart and, if possible, their arms out to the sides. If this is not possible, ask them to lie in a similar position.

Taking the rod from the left-hand side at floor level, wind it gently around the side of the person (it should not necessarily touch them) and stop at the crown. Visualise a blue colour around the person and concentrate on asking for healing energies for them. After a moment or so, gently take the rod down the other side, stopping again at ground level. Try to make sure your free hand is pointing towards the ground.

You may be aware of a particular area causing concern. In this case, making sure you have one hand pointed to the earth, pass over this area with the rod and again envisage blue or white light.

If you are already engaged in healing of some kind and are sensitive to healing energies, pass your hands over the body to scan for areas that need healing and use the rod to work on the problem, putting your other hand on the other side of the body to increase the flow of energy. You may even feel pain in your own body in the area requiring healing, but if this doesn't happen to you, don't worry. Similarly, you may be able to see auras around people. If you can, use this extra information to aid in the healing process.

All this will take several minutes. When you feel you have done all you can in the session, take the rod from the right side of the body over the top of the crown, pausing as before to envisage the blue light, and down the other side, ending at the feet. Make sure you then take the rod back up the body and end at the crown area. It is important to circle the person a maximum of three times only.

After the healing session, if your own arms feel heavy when you raise them, take the rod and shake it behind you, making sure that the free hand is always pointing towards the ground.

Chakra healing

Chakras are the source of physical, emotional, mental and spiritual energy, and using crystals with the chakras can have a great healing effect. All chakras relate to colours and to planets or the Sun and Moon.

Chakras can easily become blocked – by stresses and strains, and emotional and physical problems – and it is important to check for such blockages when carrying out healing. Crystal healing removes the blockages, allowing the body's vital energy to flow freely.

Each chakra, while separate, does link with the others. As with a pair of scales where one side balances the other, one chakra should be balanced with another, as I explain in the descriptions below. Blockages in these areas are caused by negative energies. Each chakra centre vibrates at a different rate.

It is said that, when working with crystals and the chakra centres, it is best to make sure that the person is facing the magnetic north. This can prove difficult, as not everyone will be aware which way is north, unless they have a compass.

If you are unsure whether a chakra centre is balanced after working with it, leave an appropriate stone on it (carnelian is excellent in this respect) and continue with the healing. If at any time you are in doubt as to which stone to use for chakra clearing, again carnelian is the best bet, as it directs energy to the appropriate area.

1st chakra

At the base of the spine, near to the reproductive organs, the 1st chakra (the **base chakra** or **root chakra**) sits on the coccyx. The colour of this chakra is red, its planet is Mars and it is said to relate to earth (rather than fire, as would be assumed by the Mars connection). Its stones are garnet, ruby and red coral. Haematite and jasper, with their earthy colours, are also sometimes used, while some therapists consider smoky quartz is a good crystal to use when trying to clear a blockage in this chakra.

This chakra relates to sexual activity and emotions, and is also connected with the sense of smell, as it links to our animal instincts. Sometimes it is called the 'survival chakra', because it is linked to basic instincts to survive. Associated with the adrenal glands, which are situated above the kidneys, the base chakra affects the kidneys and bladder (all connected with elimination of waste and toxins from the system), spine and skeletal bones, and is affected by fear, anger and sexual drive. Often a blockage in this chakra will manifest itself in back problems. A well-balanced base chakra will bring direction and contentment.

This chakra should be balanced with the crown chakra (the 7th chakra).

Clearing a blockage in the area requires the visualisation of white light entering the body at this point, with the crystal either directed towards the area or placed upon it.

2nd chakra

The 2nd chakra (the **spleen chakra** or **sacral chakra**) is located in the lower abdomen, just below the navel. The colour of this chakra is orange. It relates to the Sun, and to water and the feminine side of each of us. Its stones are carnelian, orange jasper and orange coral. Orange calcite is another good stone for trying to clear a blockage in this chakra.

This chakra relates to digestive problems, the release of adrenalin into the system, and the sense of taste. It is associated with the ovaries and testes, as it affects the function of the reproductive system, also the lower back, legs and feet. Often said to cover happiness, freedom and openness, this chakra makes us sensitive to the needs of other people. People actively working with and trying to help others should regularly clear this chakra centre.

Men having problems with their prostate gland should have crystal healing on this chakra as well as the base chakra.

Problems in this area can manifest themselves in loss of self-esteem and lack of motivation. This chakra balances with the throat chakra (the 5th chakra).

Clearing the 2nd chakra involves circling the area in a clockwise direction with the crystal pointed downwards slightly. Visualisation of a white light coming from the stone to this point is important.

3rd chakra

The 3rd chakra (the **solar plexus chakra** or **hara chakra**) is located at the level of the navel in the middle of the abdomen. The colour of this chakra is yellow, its planet is Mercury, and its stones are topaz, citrine and amber. Other stones that work well to clear blockages in this area are rutilated quartz, tiger's eye and malachite. This chakra links with the element of fire.

This chakra is closely connected to external stimuli. It affects the pancreas, stomach, intestines, liver and spleen and balances with the heart chakra (the 4th chakra).

Deep emotional blockages occur frequently in this area and people with blockages here often have emotional problems and lack motivation, self-esteem and energy. As Mercury is connected with communication, people with blockages in this area are often those who need to communicate as part of their life – writers especially. Blockages in this chakra can occur through repression of anger and/or subordination, and manifest themselves in kidney or liver problems. Increasing the level of activity of the person concerned can help to clear blockages in this chakra. Often problems with this chakra need time and patience to clear.

To clear this chakra with crystals, the same process is used as for clearing the base chakra.

4th chakra

The 4th chakra (the **heart chakra**) is located in the centre of the chest and connected to the thymus gland. The colour of this chakra is predominantly green, although rose is occasionally mentioned. Its planet is Venus (connected with love) and its stones are emerald, green tourmaline, green calcite, aventurine, chrysoberyl and chrysoprase. As rose also features in this chakra, rose quartz, rhodochrosite and pink tourmaline are also connected with it. This chakra links with the air and is connected to breathing in and the ability of the lungs to nourish the body with oxygen.

The thymus gland is connected to the immune system and problems in this area can lead to a lowering of immunity from infection. This chakra interacts with the adrenal glands, affecting blood, circulation, lower lungs and breasts.

This chakra is the centre of love and emotions, and blockages in this area manifest themselves in a lack of love, of self and of others. It is much affected by self-cognition, awareness and expression of love, and the imposition of others' views. It is very hard to learn to love everyone and everything unconditionally, and therefore most of us, either permanently or occasionally, will suffer from a blockage in this chakra. Someone who is often angry or judgemental may well be subject to a blockage in this area. A well-balanced heart chakra gives compassion and understanding.

To clear a blockage in this chakra, it is best to hold the crystal a few inches away from the body and, again, visualise a white light coming from the stone directly to the point concerned.

5th chakra

The 5th chakra (the **throat chakra** or **thyroid chakra**) is in the throat area, just below the vocal cords, and is connected to sound. Its colour is blue, it relates to the Moon, its stones are aquamarine, turquoise, blue topaz and blue lace agate, and it also connects with space. Some therapists suggest using lapis lazuli for this area, but I would disagree. Lapis is much better used on the 6th chakra.

Associated with the thyroid gland, the 5th chakra affects the pharynx, larynx, gums, tongue, upper lungs, shoulders, arms and hands, as well as the lymphatic system. Blockages often manifest themselves in lung problems, catarrh and sometimes eye problems. The correct functioning of this chakra is affected by mental states, and people with blockages in this area often find themselves unable to express themselves properly, probably as a result of being suppressed by others. Stress, anxieties, hidden emotions and fears can also block this chakra. A well-balanced chakra will bring about open-mindedness, good communication, creativity and self-expression.

As this chakra is connected to sound, it is possible to use sound when working on clearing a blockage. Many people suggest that mantras helps, while others suggest music. To clear a blockage with crystals, place the stone a little way from the centre and, again, visualise white light.

6th chakra

Located between the eyebrows, the 6th chakra (the **brow chakra** or **third eye chakra**) is connected with indigo, the planet Jupiter and the stones sapphire, lapis lazuli, sodalite, purple fluorite, azurite and amethyst.

Related to matters psychic or spiritual, this chakra is associated with the higher functions of the mind, the pituitary gland, the hypothalamus, the frontal lobes, one or both eyes (usually the left), the ears and the sinuses.

This chakra is the co-ordinating chakra for all the others and is affected by the desire to be open-minded.

Fear is one sign that this chakra is blocked, and when all is well in this chakra, the person is less affected by worry and doubts. Headaches and vision problems also indicate a blockage.

To clear a blockage in this chakra, the crystal should be held a few inches away from the area, pointing downwards, and should be rotated gently in a clockwise direction for several minutes.

7th chakra

Located at the top of the head, the 7th chakra (the **crown chakra**) has violet, gold and white as its colours. It is connected with the planet Saturn and with the stones amethyst, sugilite, diamond, gold fluorite and clear crystal quartz.

This chakra concerns spiritual desires and is associated with cerebral functions. Often people who suffer seasonal depression (SAD) have blockages in this area.

A well-balanced crown chakra brings about perfect awareness and enlightenment, whereas a blocked one creates a selfish and negative person. Many people would do well to work more with this chakra, as it is connected with total oneness with the universe and with nature.

This chakra balances with the base chakra (the 1st chakra) and when properly open will bring about creativity, happiness and a feeling of being at peace and in good health.

To clear a blockage in this chakra, point the crystal down towards the top of the head, turning it in clockwise circles and again visualising white light. This may take some time, and you may find your arm begins to ache. Should this happen, sit quietly with the crystal and continue the meditation for a while longer.

Working with pendulums

Dowsing with a pendulum is really easy. Most people start with a piece of either quartz crystal or amethyst, on a thong. Watch which way the pendulum swings on questions requiring a 'Yes' or 'No' answer, where you already know the answer. This will tell you how your pendulum indicates 'Yes' and 'No'. Normally speaking, the three possible movements for the pendulum are: left to right, right to left, or in a circular pattern. After finding the movement for a 'Yes' response, ask for a 'No' response and a 'Don't know' response – again by asking questions to which you know the answers.

You can use the pendulum to answer questions on vitamin deficiencies, allergies and any health problem requiring a 'Yes' or 'No' answer, but one of the easiest ways to use the pendulum is in chakra work. Simply watching how the pendulum swings will give you the answer to the question of blockages, using the Yes/No technique already discussed.

To do this sort of work, hold the pendulum in one hand and touch a chakra point with your other hand. Asking whether this chakra is blocked or not, watch which way the pendulum swings. By repeating this for each chakra point, you will be sure to find the answer to where there is a blockage. Working then to clear the chakra as discussed above will provide the healing needed.

Crystal meditation

If you want to use crystals for meditational healing, and have not done so before, start with amethyst. It is a powerful stone and a good and gentle healer, especially useful in treating nervous conditions and anxiety. Another powerful stone is quartz crystal and you may progress on to use aquamarine. Whatever you choose, the stone or stones you use must be programmed for crystal meditational healing only.

Before beginning any form of healing with crystals by meditation, make sure you ask for protection for yourself and the other person, as well as for the crystal.

Some people using crystal meditation for healing merely place a very large crystal in the room, between the 'patient' and helper; others suggest placing a small tray of crystals between patient and helper. It is equally acceptable for both parties to meditate with separate crystals.

If you are working alone to heal another person, try to link with the crystal and with them. Sit facing each other, thinking of good and imagining healing energies being directed to the area causing the concern. Close your eyes and ask the other person to do likewise, gently relax into the meditation and concentrate on the white healing light being directed to the problem area.

Sessions like this should last up to 20 minutes maximum. The main emphasis should be on trying to be at peace with the crystal, and it is important afterwards to thank the crystal for its help.

Often people get together in a group to meditate with crystals for healing. If you are about to form such a group, try to nominate someone to be in charge of the stones, care for them and cleanse them. Ideally the crystals should be placed in the middle of a circle and meditation commence after that. This creates a balanced energy.

Aura healing

The aura is the body's own energy pattern, visible outside the body. Some people are able to see auras easily, while others are not so fortunate. Not seeing someone's aura should not indicate to you that it isn't there – only that you are unable to see it.

Working on the aura is very effective; all that is necessary is a true intent to heal and help and a strong healing crystal. Again, amethyst is a good crystal to start with.

Holding the crystal in your left hand (even if you are right-handed), pass it gently around the aura of the person concerned. If you are sensitive to such things, you may find yourself stopping or slowing down in a particular area. This could indicate a break in the aura at that point. Should this happen, visualise the crystal sending energies out to heal the break and continue to cover the whole of the aura. No contact with the body is necessary and this healing only needs to be carried out a maximum of twice weekly.

This method can also be used in cases of specific physical injury. Pass the crystal over the injured area, asking for healing energies to be released by the crystal into the aura at that point.

3

stones for
healing

We will look now at 15 of the major healing stones, discussing, where applicable, traditional and modern thought on their healing properties. We will also consider elixir oils made from crystals and gemstones.

First, however, I should mention the placebo effect, which sceptics raise at every possible opportunity. A placebo has the appearance of a medicine, but has no active ingredient to affect the body; and yet it can still have a beneficial effect on the person taking it. This is the placebo effect. The assertion is that people feel better after treatment because they expect that they will, even if the medicine or healing they are receiving is worthless. Sometimes the placebo effect has been cited as the only reason for any noticeable improvement in health when crystal therapy is employed. When somebody says to me that crystal healing is 'all in the mind', I point out that many problems start in the mind and spread to the body.

The information in the following pages is based on current thought on the healing qualities of the 15 stones I most often work with. Crystal therapists do not all use the stones listed here. Many therapists compile different lists, based on the work they undertake and the results they achieve. It is up to the individual to decide which of these stones to use and which to leave out.

Amazonite

This powerful stone is pale blue-green and has a trace of copper in it. It is said to help with nervous problems and mental anguish, and is sometimes referred to as the 'Amazon stone'. It is a feldspar mineral, believed by crystal therapists to have particularly good powers of repairing the body. It comes from Brazil and is said to provide strength, help soothe the nerves and give added auric healing – thus it is often used in healing the aura, providing emotional help and support in times of trouble. Those engaged in creative work will often find this gemstone of use, as it is said to help provide perspective and rid the system of negativities. I always think of Amazonite as one of the major stones for emotional and mental problems.

Amazonite was valued greatly by the Egyptians. It is not expensive, and is relatively easy to obtain.

Amethyst

We have already mentioned this especially powerful spiritual stone. Said by some New Age followers to be less powerful than fluorite, which also carries the purple ray, amethyst is, in my opinion, an essential part of any crystal or gemstone collection, whether used for healing, self-help or meditational purposes. The amethyst belongs with the quartz family and the purple colour in the stone is due to small traces of iron.

Linking with the zodiac (see Chapter 6), this stone is often used for helping to gain psychic knowledge. It gives protection to those who wear and use it, and Christian crusaders often attached it to their rosaries in this belief. I always have a piece of polished amethyst on my person, in jewellery or on a pendulum, and I have several pieces, of various sizes, in my collection of stones for healing.

Healers in times gone by suggested that this stone could help in dream revelation, as discussed in Chapter 2, and you could try this for yourself (be sure to use a smooth piece). Many claim that it will help with inspired dreams and give clarity of thought if put under the pillow at night, or that, attached by gauze to the wrist, it will relieve insomnia and bring peace and harmony. Amethyst can help with a wide variety of problems, as it is a spiritual stone that inspires the healing of all the organs and brings about mental peace.

I always think of amethyst as a stone of love, not only human love but divine love. If we learn to love ourselves and others unconditionally, we will all experience a greater sense of well-being.

Aquamarine

This is another stone used in cases of nervous problems. The stone is 'of the sea', as its name reflects, and I have found it works especially well with people who are water signs in the zodiac, or who have a strong connection with the sea or maritime affairs. This beautiful blue-green beryl can, unfortunately, be heat-treated to make it bluer, so be sure when purchasing it that you are getting the untreated stone. Beware also of stones that look like aquamarine which are in fact spinel or glass. It is always important to buy your stones from a reputable supplier who knows and understands about gems and crystals.

I have tried taking pieces of aquamarine into exams with me and have usually found that I feel more at ease with the stone than without it. If you have an exam coming up, this is surely worth a try.

This stone can also help with stomach and thyroid problems. Especially powerful if used in meditation for such problems, this stone will help to cleanse the body and can also be effective in cases of migraine. However, as it is a particularly powerful meditational stone, it should only be used by people who are sufficiently practised in meditation to be able to cope with working at a deeper level.

The stone's connection with the sea is extended to suggest that it is useful for fluid retention problems. I have tried this with a considerable degree of success, especially for people born under the sign of Cancer the Crab, which links with water and also the moon, the latter controlling the ebb and flow of the tides. Further information on the zodiac link with this stone appears in Chapter 6.

Calcite

This is an excellent stone to use in cases of fear and anxiety. It is often used to help people who suffer badly with stress-related problems and emotional disorders. The deep-blue calcite is used widely for deep healing, blue being a particularly good healing colour. Calcite can also be white, yellow, red, green, brown, black, transparent and grey.

True calcite can be cut easily with a knife, as it is a relatively soft stone, and is commonly known as 'alabaster'. Calcite is found in large quantities in Egypt and was used by the ancient Egyptians. It is also known as limestone, marble and chalk.

Calcite helps with kidney problems. Alongside snakeskin jasper, it is often used for skin problems. Calcite is another very good meditational stone, and I can definitely recommend its use in this type of work.

Carnelian

Another stone with a zodiac link, carnelian, with its red colour stemming from iron oxides, is said to help with blood disorders and the elimination of waste products and toxins from the body. It is a powerful healer, helping to restore any broken links between the physical body and the spiritual body, and it is therefore widely used in auric healing. It is also often used in chakra balancing, when there is doubt as to whether the chakra is balanced or not. It is a 'thinking stone' and helps to focus the mind on any project requiring concentration.

In the past carnelian was used to help stop nosebleeds and soften anger. It was thought by Muslims to fulfil all desires. King Alphonso X of Spain believed it improved voice projection.

Nowadays the stone is more commonly used to help people with stress-related problems to be 'grounded' and balanced. Some texts suggest that it can be used as a tonic for the blood, but I am unable to comment on this, as I have never used it for that purpose.

I have often used this stone in meditation, as its warm red colouring helps in relaxation and focuses the mind.

Citrine

I always think of citrine with its bright yellow tones as a stone of communication. This yellow quartz is fairly rare in its pure state and may be difficult to obtain. Outlets with lots of citrine for sale may in fact be dealing with an artificially produced product, as it is possible to turn amethyst yellow by heat treatment. To tell the difference, look closely at the stone. Natural citrine will be cool and pale and seem to have a greenish tint to the yellow colouring. Artificially produced citrine will exhibit red, or even orange, shades within its depths.

Many people at some point find they need help to communicate effectively, at work, in personal relationships or merely in a general sense. I have found that citrine helps with this. The yellow colour is a natural reviver, and the citrine will help promote a feeling of self-esteem, which in turn will aid communication.

I know of crystal therapists who use this stone to help people find their true path in life. There are few people who go all through life with a sense of purpose and, if you feel that you need some direction yourself, you may wish to try using the citrine, particularly in meditation, as it could help re-establish the link between your conscious and subconscious minds. If you are feeling down, try holding a citrine for a while, as it will help lift your spirits.

Fluorite

Thought by many to be the most important healing stone for the Age of Aquarius, fluorite is indeed a powerful gemstone. It was overlooked for many years, although it was a favourite with ancient civilisations – pieces of fluorite were excavated in the ruins of Pompeii.

In more recent times, it has been heralded as the symbol of the growth of humanity and a strengthener of bone tissue. As such, it is often thought to be beneficial to women suffering from osteoporosis.

Blue John, mined in Derbyshire, England, is a form of fluorite, and it comes in varying colours, from deep, dark purple, to pink, green, yellow and blue, depending upon its source. As it is very easily scratched, it is seldom used in jewellery.

Fluorite is definitely a stone whose colours influence the way it is used but, broadly speaking, it is a repairer and builder. Many people suggest that the purple variety is as useful in healing as amethyst.

Fluorite will help bring peace and calm to a troubled mind, and holding even a very small piece in the hand can bring about a sense of calm. It is particularly useful in meditation and will help to calm even the most excitable person and promote a feeling of inner peace.

Pink fluorite will be expensive but other forms are relatively cheap.

Lapis lazuli

Sometimes also called 'lazurite', lapis lazuli has strong Egyptian, Sumerian and Biblical links, its name stemming partly from the Arabic word for 'blue' and partly from the Latin for 'stone'. It is said to be useful for people suffering from insomnia.

Its dark-blue colour with specks of gold can lead to its being confused with azurite and lazulite, which are different minerals entirely. Sodalite, which is another blue stone, can be made to look like lapis, as can jasper if dyed correctly, chalcedony and synthetic ultramarine. Glass or even plastic are sometimes passed off as lapis.

A popular healing stone for several centuries, lapis should, in my opinion, be used with care. It is extremely powerful and can lead to problems for those not able to cope with its properties.

In ancient times, it was used to cure skin problems and blood disorders. In more modern times it has been used as a healer for many diseases, from eyesight problems to fevers. Lapis lazuli is another good meditational stone, which helps to strengthen the body and promotes self-assurance.

Some people seem to have a natural affinity with lapis lazuli, and if this applies to you, you will find it will help to develop any psychic abilities you may have and increase your sensitivity. It is for this reason also that I recommend that lapis be used with care. I am particularly sensitive to lapis lazuli, and even holding a small piece for a minute will produce heightened sensitivity which can, if I'm not careful, lead to headaches and other such problems. As it can help to create a stronger bond between the spiritual and physical, it is a very good healing stone and is often used in cases of depression.

Obsidian

Obsidian is a natural glass formed from volcanic lava, usually black, hard, shiny and strong and used by many ancient civilisations for healing. The Aztecs used it to make knives, spears and arrowheads.

Obsidian can sometimes be brown/red in colour, and snowflake obsidian has white flecks.

Professional crystal therapists usually recommend balancing obsidian with a lighter crystal, such as snowy quartz, for use in healing. It is not recommended for use in absent healing. Used for relieving stomach problems and clearing the mind, it helps to balance confusion when combined with snowy quartz, as it represents the material or earth aspect of activity whereas snowy quartz represents spiritual activity.

Obsidian is sometimes used as the basis for 'magic mirrors', which are used for obtaining images in much the same way as a crystal ball. The stone is often considered to be a tool towards spiritual awareness. Gazing into even a small piece of obsidian can be a wonderful experience. It has indescribable depth, and only personal practice will enable you to fully understand its powers.

Pyrite

Often termed 'fool's gold', pyrite is frequently used in making jewellery, when it is passed off as marcasite, although true marcasite is quite different and less adaptable.

Mexican Indians used pyrite, rather than obsidian, for their magic mirrors. Professional crystal therapists use the stone extensively on any addiction problems. It allows the person to connect with the earth's energy and is said to help strengthen the will.

Modern usage seems to be directed mainly towards lung or breathing problems, as well as digestive disorders and depression.

Quartz crystal

Quartz crystal is one of the three most important stones for healing, the other two being amethyst and fluorite. Said to generate and amplify electricity passing from the healer to the patient, quartz unblocks energy centres and helps the body to heal itself. Having achieved a state of well-being, many therapists suggest that simply holding a piece of quartz crystal each day will help to boost the immune system and stave off future illness. It should be noted, however, that mineralogists suggest that quartz neither conducts nor amplifies electricity. Quartz crystal is a valuable aid in self-healing and can be used in single point or cluster form. Many programmer or generator crystals are clusters of quartz crystal.

When referring to 'crystal', many therapists mean quartz crystal. I use the term 'quartz crystal' to refer to clear quartz. Other coloured varieties (such as rose quartz) are referred to separately.

There are many types of coloured quartz in addition to rose quartz: for example, snowy quartz, smoky quartz, rutilated quartz (which can be clear or smoky), citrine, amethyst, tourmalinated quartz and aventurine.

About an eighth of the world's crust is quartz, and it has been used in buildings for thousands of years. Many ancient people mistakenly believed clear quartz to be fossilised ice. Roman ladies used to carry quartz balls around to cool their hands when the weather turned warm. American Indians used quartz for divining, and other ancient peoples used the stone for cauterising wounds.

The greatest use for quartz crystal is in meditation. It is excellent when used in deep meditations, as it seems to help the mind to focus. Its main usage should perhaps be to help heal the mind rather than the body, although many therapists use it when carrying out chakra healing, as it is said to dispel negativities.

Rose quartz

Rose quartz ranks alongside amethyst in my personal preference list. Its beautiful, gentle, pink shade seems to have a healing quality in its own right. The stone is usually found in chunks, as it does not form individual crystals.

An important stone in chakra healing, rose quartz seems to deal with the heart and with love and emotions. Holding a piece of this stone invariably leads to a feeling of inner peace, and people suffering from trauma would be well directed to sit with a piece of rose quartz, and perhaps enter into meditation, if they feel comfortable with this.

As a calming stone, it exposes emotional imbalances. It is said that a piece of rose quartz in a room where tensions are likely to rise will stop matters reaching boiling point. I have tried this on occasions, sometimes with success.

As the stone is useful in reducing high blood pressure, some therapists suggest that it is beneficial in dealing with heart problems and as a diuretic. Others are more specific, suggesting it helps the kidney area and stimulates the circulation. I cannot comment on this, as I have yet to try the stone in this connection, but I can say that rose quartz is very good to use for emotional problems and is exceptionally effective in meditation and as a stress-reducer. I have used it in the treatment of headaches and migraines, which may be stress-related.

Sodalite

Sodalite is a lovely blue stone, sometimes peppered with white calcite. It is helpful for those who suffer with anxieties and nervous problems. Said to balance the mind, it helps people who are highly strung to be a little more focused and rational. It is another stone believed to lower blood pressure.

People who suffer with nervous trouble may well wish to wear it regularly, especially in situations that they think may prove stressful.

Sodalite may also help promote communication and encourages forms of self-expression.

A piece of sodalite under the pillow may help you remember your dreams.

Tiger's eye

A member of the quartz family, tiger's eye is golden yellow and brown. It is often polished to make tumble stones, eggs, beads and pyramids and makes eye-catching jewellery.

For years, I have carried a piece of tiger's eye around in my purse. The reason is that it helps to counteract nervous or stress-related illnesses, increases self-confidence and benefits the digestive system. It is also said to give those who carry it clearer perception and is particularly useful in business dealings.

Popular with people who study Chinese philosophies, this stone, with its layers of dark next to bright colouring, seems to be the epitome of the Yin/Yang principle – i.e. the principle of male and female, or negative and positive, working together in harmony.

Meditating with this stone should be left until the art of meditation at a deep level has been attained.

Tourmaline

Tourmaline gets its name from the Sinhalese *turmalli*, which means 'mixed precious stone', and indeed no other gemstone has so many colourings and varieties. It can be brown, orange, green, blue, black, dark green, yellow and many other colours. One stone can have as many colours within it as you care to name.

Watermelon tourmaline has a blue/green outer layer and is pink/red inside. This form is particularly good for meditation, although claims that it can alter the structure of cells are probably false.

Said to benefit those suffering with nervous problems, especially if worn against or close to the skin, tourmaline is sometimes known as the 'confidence stone', as it helps dispel fear and negativities and helps those using it to face adversity. It is particularly useful in dealing with mental anguish, possibly because of its wonderful colourings.

We have now covered what, in my opinion, are the 15 main healing stones. As you will have gathered, certain claims for the healing properties of the stones may be over-ambitious, but I leave it to the individual to carry out his or her own research into the stones and decide in which way to use each crystal or gemstone. Remember: doctors are the proper people to treat physical illness. Crystal therapy complements, but does not replace, orthodox medicine.

Gemstone elixirs and oils

Now we will look briefly at gemstone elixirs and massage oils. Gem elixirs are usually made from water in which the relevant stone has been soaked. They can be used as a means of drawing the healing vibrations of the crystals into the body.

Making your own elixir

It is possible to make up your own gem elixir using filtered water that has been sterilised and purified. It is best not to use bottled water, as it may have been irradiated. Put your gemstone in the water and leave it in the sun for four hours. You should always use a stone that has been programmed for healing purposes and also perhaps programmed to work within a gem elixir. It is said that the best time to make an elixir is the two hours either side of midday. Remove the stones and pour the elixir into 10 ml bottles, filling two thirds of the bottle. Fill the other third with pure alcohol (vodka is acceptable). Label and shake the bottles occasionally to prevent stagnation. The shelf-life of elixir is only three months.

It is possible to make an elixir using more than one stone, and if you are thinking of doing this, try to use a carnelian as they are excellent for gem elixirs. They seem to direct the energy to the most appropriate place for healing. If in doubt which stone to use for your elixir, carnelian (the thinking stone) is the best one to use.

If you feel you need a gem elixir quickly and have not had time to make one (say you have had only two hours rather than the four required), it is possible to speed up the process by placing the bottle or elixir in a glass on a cluster or within a crystal triangulation (three crystals in a triangular shape).

Taking the elixir

You need to be in a calm and relaxed state to use a gem elixir. It is recommended that you take a few deep breaths and hold the bottle before actually taking the elixir. Then place three or four drops in the mouth, preferably under the tongue. Three drops of the gem elixir can be placed in a cup of tea to relieve stress and depression. It should be taken at least 30 minutes before or after a meal.

Citrine and aventurine are said to lift the energy of a person, while yellow and red calcite and turritella agate will lift a person's confidence and self-esteem. A note of caution – don't use gem elixirs too often, as doing so can cause over-stimulation. Occasional use is the best advice with such potions. If you feel ill on taking an elixir, stop at once.

Elixir oils

Elixir oils, similar to aromatherapy oils, are another form of treatment. The skin absorbs the oil which helps the body open up to the healing vibrations of the stone.

To make an elixir oil, use any natural oil, vegetable, nut or fruit. Cold-pressed, virgin olive oil is a good releaser of blockages. Most therapists suggest grapeseed oil as the best carrier, because it is good for skin cleansing and helps eliminate toxins. Wheatgerm oil is another good carrier and especially good for damaged skin. Most aromatherapists will suggest sweet almond oil, as it is very easily absorbed, non-greasy and an excellent healing oil.

Place the stones directly into the oil, avoiding contamination from dirt. Charge your oil elixir under a pyramid shape or in a triangle made by three crystals. It is said that moonlight-charged elixirs can be used for emotional problems with good results and that leaving elixirs in the moonlight will also help with fluid-retention problems (again relating back to the waxing and waning of the moon and its effects on the tide). Amethyst is a good stone to use for stress and tension, and rock quartz will help with back problems. An elixir oil made of wheatgerm and aventurine is said to be good for stretch marks, if used twice daily.

Before applying the elixir oil, use the thumb and palms to warm and stimulate the skin. Use the palms to apply the oil initially and massage gently.

Do not take gem elixir oils internally. They are for massage purposes only.

everyday
health

I believe that we can help our bodies to heal themselves and that our mental approach affects healing. It is essential to trust any therapy given, by your doctor and by your crystal and gemstone therapist. In this chapter we will look at the use of crystals, and self-help measures, in treating some particular health problems.

Crystal and gemstone therapy should not replace medication or medical advice from your doctor. Crystal and gemstone therapy can help speed healing but if your complaint continues, it is always best to consult your doctor. In that way, this form of healing can complement the medication and advice given to you.

The term 'alternative therapy' is often used for any treatment other than the conventional medical help available from doctors, but I feel this gives a wrong impression that orthodox medical help can be dismissed as unnecessary. Chiropractic, acupuncture, herbalism, homoeopathy and naturopathy might be called 'alternative therapy', but gemstone and crystal therapy is better described as 'complementary therapy'. There is a place for complementary therapies alongside orthodox forms of healing.

Treating physical complaints

Migraines

One of the commonest complaints, especially among people who are subjected to high levels of stress, is the type of headache called 'migraine' – headaches with neurological symptoms, such as numbness, distorted vision or weakness down one side of the body.

Although stress is one of the main causes of migraines, they can be related to diet, and cheese, coffee, chocolate and other foods often lead to an attack. Women taking oral contraceptives may also find they become prone to migraines, and if this is the case, the doctor should be informed.

Treatment

Self-help measures obviously include cutting down, or even cutting out, any dietary substance that may trigger an attack, and trying to be aware of potentially stressful situations and to deal with them calmly.

The stones most commonly used to help with migraines are jet, aventurine and rose quartz. These can be used by working on the brow chakra, as discussed earlier, or by merely holding the stone on the forehead and taking deep breaths. A few drops of elixir oil may also be massaged on to the temples and stomach to ease the problem. Auric healing may also be of help.

I have found it is best to use these treatments as early as possible before the full-blown migraine develops. After an acute migraine has developed, however, the therapies using crystals and gemstones can still help, but should be combined with rest in a darkened room.

Depression

There are few things more generally debilitating than depression. Some people suffer such severe depression that they have to seek psychiatric help. It should be understood here that we do not attempt to help people who suffer with manic depression or a serious depressive disorder, or those who are suffering from post-natal depression. People with these problems should be directed to their doctor and only when the situation begins to improve should they seek help from crystals and gemstones. Any depression that lasts more than a few weeks always needs the help of a doctor.

Treatment
Emerald, jasper, smoky quartz and occasionally zircon are the most common crystals and gemstones for dealing with depression. Amethyst, aquamarine (especially for nervous depression), tourmaline and fluorite can also help, and I always feel it is best to offer the person to be treated a variety of stones, allowing them to choose one they feel comfortable with personally.

In addition to crystal and gemstone therapy, people suffering from depression would be well advised to take more exercise. Depression can often stem from bottled-up stress and emotion, which can be released through exercise lasting more than 20 minutes.

Sometimes it is also useful to keep a diary, to talk things over with people who are willing to listen and to learn to express pent-up emotions and anxieties. Professional crystal therapists often deal with people who are suffering from depression and are more than willing to listen to the problems being experienced. Many professional crystal therapists use the ruby on an initial visit, putting it on the heart or base chakra centres.

Learning to relax is very important in overcoming depression and so meditation, with any of the crystals discussed in Chapter 3, is likely to be of benefit. It may be helpful too to carry around the chosen crystal or gemstone, as it will then help the healing process throughout the day.

Skin problems

Skin problems include a multitude of differing ailments, such as cold sores, hives, acne, bruising, boils and pimples, eczema, psoriasis, ulcers and even skin cancers. We are concerned here with minor skin problems. Major problems must receive medical attention. Do not try to treat moles with crystals; go to your doctor. Go to your doctor if any symptoms persist.

Treatment

Many skin complaints, such as blisters and boils, benefit from exposure to air and simply being kept clean, and this should be the first course of action with such problems. Boils in particular can be a sign of stress, as they usually appear when a person is run-down or weakened by a poor diet. Anything, therefore, that can aid relaxation will be of benefit.

Elixir oils may help with these types of skin complaints and should be used with gentle massage. An elixir oil made from snakeskin jasper is very good for the skin.

Cold sores are caused by the herpes simplex virus which often lies dormant in people, to appear at times of stress or fever. Taking extra B complex vitamin often helps with cold sores and using an oil or one made with wheatgerm oil may also help.

With regard to other skin problems, agate, aventurine, cat's-eye, red coral and sapphire may aid in the healing process and can be used either as elixir oils or alone by placing the gemstone or crystal on the area in question and seeking healing in that way. Cat's-eye and red coral are said to be particularly effective for eczema. Aventurine gem elixir made with water is particularly good for minor skin irritations and should preferably be made the day before, left overnight, and then used to gently bathe the affected area. Calcite and snakeskin jasper are also often used to treat general skin problems. Amethyst cluster is often used for ruptured tissue, burns, sprains and grazed skin, and rose sand crystals are good for skin repair.

It should be remembered that skin problems may be a result of an allergy to a material, a food substance or something such as a new washing powder. It is best to eliminate these possibilities as a matter of course before commencing any form of crystal or gemstone therapy.

Rheumatism

Pain and stiffness in joints, which are the main symptoms of rheumatism, can strike at any age, although relatively more people over the age of 50 will suffer with this complaint. Always see your doctor if you suffer prolonged pain in your joints.

Treatment

One of the oldest ways to treat rheumatism is by using copper. Many people wear copper bracelets, and stones with a trace of copper may also help.

Generally speaking, however, the most popular stones for the treatment of rheumatism are lodestone, an iron oxide, or magnetite and malachite, which both contain traces of copper. Turquoise also contains copper traces, as do dioptase, chrysocolla, and azurite, and these may be tried.

Malachite made into a gemstone elixir may relieve rheumatism and a few drops can be taken in a cup of tea.

Insomnia

Insomnia, being unable to get to sleep or to stay asleep, affects almost everyone at some time. Drinking coffee, noise, worry, anxiety and pain can all lead to an inability to get to sleep.

Treatment

The ability to relax certainly plays a large part in whether a person manages to get a good night's sleep. If you are worried about something or in pain, you will not be relaxed, and therefore will be likely to experience problems in achieving the necessary state for sleep.

Taking more exercise should always be considered if insomnia becomes a problem. Other self-help measures include a warm, milky drink at night (not coffee), a warm but well-ventilated bedroom, a comfortable bed or sleeping position, and a warm bath just before retiring. Try not to eat late at night, as your sleep-pattern will be disturbed. People with a nervous disposition should avoid watching horror films or thrillers late at night. Further good advice is never to go to bed on an argument with your partner; you will lie awake thinking about what has been said, and will find it almost impossible to get to sleep. Rose quartz may help here, as it soothes emotions.

Amethyst is very effective in producing a state of relaxation and a small tumblestone of amethyst under the pillow is said to help enormously with insomnia. Other stones to consider are emerald, zircon, peridot and topaz. Diamond, with its ability to help clear the mind, may also be something to try, but could prove costly!

Respiratory problems

Many factors cause difficulties with breathing. A cold or sinus problem can make it difficult to breathe properly, as can laryngitis, tonsillitis, bronchitis and hay fever. Any form of congestion on the lungs will also make things difficult, so do see your doctor if problems persist.

Treatment

Amber is said to be particularly effective in cases of bronchial disorders and asthma; pearl in clearing catarrh and helping with lung infections; pyrite in clearing sinus congestion; and rutilated quartz in asthma and bronchitis. Turquoise may also be beneficial, as it helps with respiratory and circulatory problems.

Using gemstone elixir oils may be the best form of treatment, but some people find sufficient help from merely holding their chosen stone.

After a bout of flu or a heavy cold, or when feeling generally below par, using staurolite may help, as this stone often helps increase energy levels. Sometimes known as the 'fairy stone', it may be difficult to obtain in a pure form.

Persistent problems with breathing should always be referred to a doctor for a full medical check-up.

High blood pressure

Blood pressure readings show how hard the heart is working to pump the blood round the body. Pressure can increase or decrease, depending on the level of activity being undertaken at the time.

Treatment

High blood pressure is very common among middle-aged people leading sedentary lives and, conversely, jet-setting executives suffering stress! It can be a by-product of overeating, overdrinking, too much salt in the diet, being overweight, lack of exercise or a potential heart problem, such as the weakness of the heart or hardening of the arteries. High blood pressure can run in families, but its effects can be significantly lessened by watching the diet and exercising. Smoking should be reduced or, better still, given up, and the diet should include more fibre and reduced amounts of salt, sugar, fats, and red meat.

Anything that reduces stress should be considered. However, it would be quite wrong to suggest an immediately stringent exercise regime for someone who has previously been inactive, as the disadvantages could outweigh any advantages. Changing lifestyle gradually is much more effective than a sudden change. Relaxation and cutting down on alcohol could be enough to lower a high blood pressure reading.

The stones that may help are haematite and sodalite, both good stress-reducers. Haematite is said to help reduce a rapid pulse rate, while sodalite is often used by professional therapists to reduce high blood pressure. Taking up meditation should be considered, and meditation with either of these stones could result in a marked improvement in the condition.

Treating stress

Many other common health problems can be helped by the use of crystals, as discussed in Chapter 3, in the information on different stones. Using crystals and gemstones is often most beneficial for mental and emotional well-being, and a problem in this area that we all face at some time is stress.

When dealing with stress, one of the main difficulties is identifying the cause. There may, indeed, be more than one cause and it is vital to target all these areas if the stress is to be successfully resolved. Some matters are easier than others to deal with: for example, financial worries are unlikely to be resolved overnight, whereas stress caused by overwork can be reduced by reorganisation or reassessing the situation. A major cause of stress is the need to achieve; we often set ourselves unattainable goals and then feel stressed when we fail to achieve them. We need to give ourselves quality time alone to unwind. Gentle exercise is often a good way to reduce stress, and walking can be one of the most beneficial methods of stress-reduction.

In a stressful situation, we need to create a balance, a calm, which will help to release any pent-up emotions. Learning to relax is the first step to reducing stress levels. Meditation, especially with crystals and gemstones (as discussed in Chapter 2), may be the answer to creating the necessary balance. If you feel under a lot of stress, try a simple meditation of 15 minutes or so, possibly using amethyst or rose quartz. You may also wish to consider massage with gem elixir oils. Quietly receiving a gentle massage, perhaps with soft background music, can be very therapeutic, and the added help of the gemstones and crystals can make it very relaxing indeed.

Other crystals and gemstones known to be good to use for stress include agate, celestite, chrysoprase, garnet, rhodochrosite, tourmaline, alexandrite, dioptase, kunzite and onyx.

Stress reduction during sleep

Using crystals to help with sleep may also help reduce stress. A growing number of doctors now think that the greatest percentage of healing takes place while we are asleep, because our mind is not active and our body is allowed to heal itself.

To use crystals during sleep, programme your stone for the purpose, asking for healing, and strap it to your wrist (most authorities suggest the left wrist) with gauze. Alternatively, use a small tumblestone placed under your pillow; however, contact with the crystal or gemstone is considered to be most beneficial. In addition, in the daytime, you may wish to wear your chosen stone, which should not be the actual stone used during the sleep process but another stone of the same kind. Again, this stone should be programmed for healing. Then, when situations become exceptionally stressful, you can take time out on your own and give yourself a gentle massage in the temple area or sit and hold the stone and enter into a short meditation, asking for help and healing at the same time.

Carrying a gemstone

You can carry around your healing stone in a variety of ways. Some people wear theirs as jewellery. Others make a 'crystal pouch' which can be sewn inside a garment and detached easily when the clothing needs washing. Remember, though, that the stone will also need regular washing, cleansing, clearing and reprogramming, because it will be subject to the same dirt and pollution as the clothes you wear.

If you decide to carry your gemstone or crystal around with you, make sure you touch it regularly, to reinforce the special bond. Think of it as a friend and companion and it will serve you well. Make sure that you let it see and feel sunlight. I make a point of talking to my stones, both those I carry around with me and those I have at home. If I have a problem, I tell my crystals, especially the one I carry around with me to help me in day-to-day situations; I ask the stone for help, telling it why and what I would ideally like from a situation.

Carrying around your own crystal or gemstone leads to a special bond. It also means that you always have a stone with you, should you have time for meditation. Meditating can make personal troubles seem far less significant and thereby reduces stress.

Healing your pets

I know of many people who have tried using crystals to help their pets, with remarkable success. To jibes from her family and friends, one lady programmed a crystal to help her dog, which suffered badly with mobility problems due to old age and arthritis. She attached the crystal inside the dog's collar, meditated regularly for healing to be given through the crystal, and regularly told the animal that he was receiving healing and would get well. Within a week or so, the dog showed a remarkable improvement. So much for the placebo effect! The dog most certainly didn't know that he was supposed to be feeling better, but the improvement was considerable.

You may also wish to try the use of gem elixirs. It is recorded that, in times gone by, farmers gave 'crystal water' (water that had been used to soak crystals) to their sick animals, offering a prayer of healing for them at the same time. Perhaps this should be re-instated. There is no reason why animals should not benefit from crystal and gemstone healing in the same way as humans.

Visiting a crystal therapist

If you visit a crystal therapist for help with one of the ailments discussed in this chapter, you should not be surprised if the therapist uses different stones from those I have mentioned in my explanations. Crystal therapists use stones with which they have experience, and in many cases, their choice of stones depends on their own preferences and intuition. Crystal therapy uses both the energy of the healer and the energy of the crystal or gemstone – so it is important to have faith both in the stone and the person carrying out the treatment.

lithomancy

In this chapter we will look at lithomancy, which means casting the stones and using the patterns in which they fall to help us with our direction in life.

I doubt whether there is anyone who never feels the need for guidance about what to do or which path to take in life. Help is offered by many so-called 'New Age' practices, including tarot, runes, I Ching, numerology, palmistry and astrology – as well as lithomancy.

If you decide to embark on lithomancy for other people, I must stress the need to be caring and considerate. When people are troubled, they are looking not only for a sympathetic ear but also for help that should be clear and concise, yet thorough. However, it is not up to the person carrying out the reading to tell the other what to do. The art is in making suggestions, offering choices and allowing the other person to choose what they consider is right for them. People must remain responsible for their actions. It is also vital to be positive in what you say; do not end the reading on a negative note. Be sincere, encouraging and helpful.

How to start

Some professionals working in this field use only five stones, while others use several more and others as many as 200. It is for the individual to decide how many stones they wish to use and in which ways they want to use and interpret them.

The crystals you use for lithomancy must be specially programmed for this purpose and used for nothing else. Ideally, they should be kept separately from healing crystals and gemstones. You should also be aware of the need for regular cleansing, as many people may touch the stones; before they can be re-used, they need to be cleansed of any negativities they have picked up.

Most people keep their stones on a tray so they can be easily seen by the person seeking help and handled properly. You will also need to consider the surface onto which the stones are to be cast. Some people use sand trays, while others use silk cloths (black shows the stones off to their best advantage). Others, who have no strong feelings on this, merely cast the stones onto a table top.

Watch to see how the person chooses the stones. Some people will just pick up stones and others will take time choosing, looking at them over and over again before making a decision. You can learn from this what sort of individual you are dealing with and whether they are rash, intuitive or logical.

If you know the star sign of the person, it is interesting to see how this relates to their choice of stones. Virgoans, for example, are likely to choose colours that co-ordinate; Arians are likely to go for bright colours and have no changes of decision at all, unlike Librans who may spend a long time choosing their stones.

Meanings of the stones

We will now look at the meaning of 31 of the gemstones and crystals. It is for you to decide whether to use all or some of these or to use a couple of the stones several times. You may, of course, decide to use others not listed here. The meanings given are traditional. Many professionals, however, may use slightly different meanings, based on intuition or psychic input, and you may be able to formulate your own meanings.

Agate

Agates indicate increases of energy and surprises, and when seen in a reading suggest that the energy of the person concerned may be put to the test in an unexpected way.

Agate quartz usually represents a young man. Many professional readers suggest this stone is the young man of the family, the son, or someone who is very close to the questioner.

An **agate with fossils** represents finances, and there are possibilities of financial improvement, should opportunities be grasped. There is also a likelihood of a win on a lottery or a legacy of some kind, as there will definitely be an increase in money.

Amethyst

This lovely, spiritual stone shows an interest in personal development or philosophy. Most people who choose an amethyst will also choose the rose quartz, as they seem to interrelate, especially for healing. Someone who selects both of these stones is likely to be interested in, or capable of, spiritual healing. Amethyst can also indicate creativity, usually for the benefit of others.

Aquamarine

Logic, rationality and clear thinking are represented by this stone, and the person choosing it may be sending out a message of lack of trust in what you are likely to say. They are in doubt about the validity of this form of self-help and may need extra persuasion that what is being said will really help them.

Beryl

People who pick the beryl are likely to be interested in spirituality, personal development, psychic powers and intuition. Should this stone appear in a reading, look to see if the amethyst and rose quartz are also present. If so, you have someone who may have a psychic talent that could be encouraged.

Bloodstone

Aches and pains, stresses and strains are usually associated with this stone when it appears in a reading. The problem could be in the past, present or future, and it is up to the reader to determine which. However, it does suggest that the questioner ought to slow down. Remember to phrase any advice of this nature in a helpful and positive way.

Blue lace agate

A young girl, probably within the family, is represented by this stone. As all agates are sensitive to other gemstones and crystals around them, it is necessary to look at the stones that surround the blue lace agate before making any firm statements. For example, should the bloodstone be next to the blue lace agate, with amethyst the other side, one could assume that there are possible health problems connected with a young girl, with which the questioner may be able to help with healing.

Citrine

A communication, usually a job offer, a new opening or a new relationship is represented by this lovely yellow stone. Again, it is necessary to look at the other stones in the area to see where this new beginning may lie.

Coral

Someone who chooses the coral is likely to have undergone a transformation of some kind in the recent past and probably come through it better and wiser than before. This can relate to job, home, family or health. Again, the reader must look to the other stones for help to decide in which area this transformation has taken place.

Fluorite

Someone who picks this stone is likely to be artistic, creative and talented in some way, and to be able to earn money from the talent, should they wish to. The person drawing this stone may be over-self-critical, fear failure and need to be convinced that their talent is worth pursuing.

Garnet

Garnets indicate good news, favourable communications, usually by post or telephone. Should the citrine be nearby, the news will probably be by telephone.

Green jasper

Rejections in love are indicated by this stone, if it is the dark-green variety. The rejection can be either in a romantic relationship or in a family situation and feelings are likely to be strong. The person concerned may feel neglected and worthless or that the love they give is not returned in the same way. This may be an actual situation or how they perceive it. Should the green jasper be light rather than dark green, there will be happiness in love and general contentment.

Jet

The drawing of this dark, black stone represents dark emotions, possible unfaithfulness and someone who is not willing to share.

This could be the questioner or someone to whom they are close. Again, it is necessary to look at the surrounding stones before making a firm decision on who this stone represents.

Labradorite

Overseas travel, links with foreign shores, holidays perhaps, are all indicated by this stone. There may be travel for business or pleasure, communication from abroad, a relationship with a foreigner, or a summer holiday to the sunshine.

Moonstone

The person who chooses this stone may have difficulty distinguishing the real from the unreal, truth from reality, and be accused of daydreaming a lot of the time. Any artistic interests should be developed. The questioner should be advised to start something new, which could be a challenge, rather than drift professionally.

Moss agate

This is one of the best stones to see in a reading. Its presence shows calm after a storm – a period of contentment after a period of anxiety and worry. If this stone appears, you can assure the questioner that things are about to improve and all will be well. There will be much to look forward to in the future.

Petrified wood

The appearance of petrified wood suggests legal papers, legal matters or the law in general. This could be advantageous or not; again, the reader must look at the surrounding stones. There could be a will, a marriage, an agreement or contract, but conversely there could also be a divorce, trouble in a business matter, or a some legal dispute.

Pink and grey jasper

While green jasper indicates a young girl, pink and grey jasper indicate older people, male or female. These could be parents or others close to the questioner who are considerably older. They will affect the questioner in some way, in hopes, plans and the future generally. There could be a legacy or an unexpected gift or an older person may have to move in with the questioner due to health or other problems.

Pyrite

Iron pyrites were often taken to be gold, by inexperienced miners; hence the nickname 'fool's gold'. The appearance of this stone in a reading indicates that all is not what it seems. There is deception or general mistrust around. The reader must use the surrounding stones to decide how to interpret pyrite. It could suggest that someone needs to be careful not to be deceived. It can also mean that someone is gullible and easily taken in. The person could be duped in a partnership or may be contemplating embarking on a venture that needs careful consideration. When anyone chooses this stone, it should be suggested that they think first and act later, rather than rush into something that may not be what it seems.

Quartz crystal

The return of good health, an increase in energy, vitality and stamina are all suggested by the presence of this crystal in a reading. If the questioner has been ill, it suggests the return of health and is a good sign. Should the questioner be a little unsure of a situation, this stone indicates a surge of energy that will take matters forward and a reliance on inner strength rather than other people. Success is suggested and achievements will be many.

Red jasper

Jaspers calm troubled emotions and troubled minds and the presence of the red jasper in a reading suggests love, passion, jealousy and deep, strong emotions, especially if a large number are chosen. These emotions will relate to other people rather than situations.

Rose quartz

This healing stone indicates that the questioner has healing capabilities, in personal, hands-on healing and absent healing; or the ability to heal spiritually, especially if the aquamarine is close by.

Ruby

Those who choose the ruby are likely to be fussy and demand perfection in everything and everybody. They often feel frustrated because they place unnecessarily high demands on themselves as well as others and feel unable to meet their self-imposed standards. They fear failure. They may be obsessive and this is something that may be mentioned. They should be advised to be easier on themselves and those close to them.

Rutilated quartz

The rutilated quartz is a lovely crystal. What appears to be a pale crystal has bright golden threads running through it. In a reading, this stone indicates artistic ability or creativity. The person who chooses it may already be earning a living from artistic pursuits; or they may be capable of doing so, perhaps not realising it and needing some persuasion to accept the talent; or they may derive a great deal of pleasure from craft or handwork.

Sapphire

Sapphires indicate happiness, peace and harmony. If they are present in a reading, there is likely to be a period of happiness and contentment, although this may be short-lived.

Sardonyx

Weddings, engagements, proposals, love affairs and romance are all indicated by this stone. Most professionals suggest that the stone means a wedding, although not necessarily for the questioner. However, I feel that the stone refers to all love interests, and should not necessarily be taken to be a wedding.

Tektite

Tektite is a dull, black or brownish-looking stone, which is actually fused glass. It does not look very appealing and is usually small. Probably formed by or from meteorites, its presence in a reading indicates a feeling of despair, depression, withdrawal or hopelessness. The person who chooses this stone may be suffering from these symptoms, although appearing cheerful. Alternatively, the presence of the stone may indicate someone in the questioner's surroundings who fits this picture. When this stone appears, see what other stones are also drawn. If most appear fairly optimistic, the depression may have passed.

Tiger's Eye

Self-confidence, independence but also loneliness are indicated by this stone's appearance. Someone very independent can also be very insular, as can someone who has had to stand up for themselves following a divorce or separation of some kind. This stone almost always indicates changes for the better, so should someone be going through a divorce, separation or other type of loss, and feeling very alone and isolated, they should be made aware that the changes taking place will be for the best in the long run; they will have learned and grown from the experience and will be wiser for it.

Topaz

The choosing of topaz suggests that there may be relationship difficulties and extreme care should be exercised, especially if the relationship is new. No firm statements should be made.

Turquoise

Anyone who draws the turquoise is likely to be a lucky person, seemingly protected from adversities. Peace, contentment and lasting happiness are assured. This is a very positive stone.

Once the stones have been chosen, ask the questioner to cast them. You then decide which layout they most closely approach. If they do not seem to fall in a pattern, ask the questioner to throw them again, and perhaps again, until they do fall into a recognisable layout. We will discuss only four layouts here. Once you have gained experience with these four, you might want to draw up your own interpretations for other patterns.

Carrying out a reading will take time to do well and you should not expect to be able to achieve this until you have practised many times. Don't forget that the meanings of the stones need to be looked at in relation to the stones thrown next to them. You should also take into account the number of times the same stone has been chosen.

The zodiac layout

Based on 12 houses, the zodiac layout will look something like this:

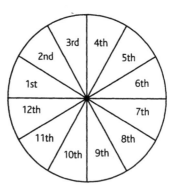

The meaning of the houses is as follows:

* **1st house**   – the questioner
* **2nd house**   – finances and material possessions
* **3rd house**   – brothers, sisters, communication, short-distance travel

* **4th house**   –   home and family life
* **5th house**   –   children or lovers
* **6th house**   –   health, jobs or family pets
* **7th house**   –   partnerships, either personal or business
* **8th house**   –   sex, birth, life and death
* **9th house**   –   long-distance travel or study
* **10th house** –   job or career, status and environment
* **11th house** –   friends, hopes and wishes, group situations
* **12th house** –   difficulties and fears

It is, of course, necessary to look at the stones chosen as a whole, and working from the 1st house through to the 12th, form a logical reading. Look at opposite houses, as well as adjacent ones, when using this reading. By exploring the meaning of each stone in each house and looking at stones in the opposite and adjacent houses, you will be able to build up a logical interpretation.

The gypsy layout

Draw a large circle on the floor. You may wish to have a circle made up of string readily available for this purpose. It should be at least 40 cm across. Thirteen stones should be chosen, plus a standard garden pebble. The questioner should take all these in his/her left hand and throw them into the circle. The pebble is said to indicate the questioner and is known as 'the significator'. Should this stone fall outside the circle and all the others inside it, the stones need to be re-thrown. Tradition stipulates that, should this happen a second time, the whole exercise should be abandoned.

You should read the meanings of each of the stones, looking particularly at their distance from the significator and also at adjacent stones.

The random nine layout

The questioner takes any nine stones from the tray. Look to see how long they take in choosing, whether they seem to change their mind, whether they look at the stones in detail or not. All these things have a bearing on the reading you will give. People who just pick up any nine stones and throw them anywhere are likely to be rash, impulsive individuals who don't think things through. Those who spend time choosing the stones, arrange them in a nice pattern, colour co-ordinate them and so on, are probably very organised, thorough, thoughtful and possibly apprehensive. Make a mental note of the stones that are picked up and then rejected – they may relate to events just passed or events with which the questioner feels uncomfortable.

Once the nine stones have been chosen, ask the questioner to lay them out however they like. Then ask yourself whether the stones lie all together in one group or in maybe two or more small groups. Are the groups all colour-related or related in another way, such as one group relating to people, another to personal circumstances?

It is always prudent to ask the questioner whether there is one area of their life that requires more attention than the others. While it is good to give as much information as you can, the questioner will possibly be waiting to hear about only one aspect in particular and will forget most of the rest of what is said.

Let's pretend we are doing a reading for a lady called Jo. She is 26, married, has two small children (both boys), and she comes to you for advice on a potential business venture. She is worried that time away from home will upset her eldest son, who is very sensitive. She decides to draw nine stones and puts them in three groups:

* **Group 1** – agate quartz, green jasper, moss agate
* **Group 2** – petrified wood, pyrite, tiger's eye
* **Group 3** – turquoise, rutilated quartz, quartz crystal

Group 1 refers to the situation regarding Jo's son (agate quartz). There is anxiety here, as shown by the green jasper, and yet the presence of the moss agate indicates that this period of anxiety is likely to be at an end. All will be well and she has been worrying about her son unnecessarily.

Group 2 refers to the setting up of a new company. Legal documents will be around (petrified wood), but she should watch what she signs (pyrite). She will need to be very independent (tiger's eye) and she may have to make headway unaided.

Group 3 refers to the future. Turquoise is a positive stone, full of hope, calm and happiness. Rutilated quartz indicates that Jo's venture may revolve around her own artistic or creative nature, and although she may refuse to acknowledge that she is good at what she does, and seldom seems to get any support from others, she is likely to do well, as the turquoise is a very positive note in a reading. The quartz crystal suggests that she will have the inner strength to see her through, be full of energy and determination and will succeed, despite her fears.

The 13 stone layout

This layout, by tradition, uses stones other than gemstones or crystals. It was described to me by someone who uses pebbles from the beach. However, it seems so good that I see no reason why it couldn't be used with gemstones and crystals.

You need 13 stones. The first seven represent Sun and Moon and the planets Mercury, Venus, Mars, Jupiter and Saturn. The other six represent situations: life and health, luck, magic, love, home and family, and news.

Each planet has a colour and it is best to use a stone that matches this colour. The seven colours are as follows, with some ideas on the types of stones to choose:

* **Sun**	–	yellow (citrine, rutilated quartz, dendritic agate)
* **Moon**	–	grey (moonstone)
* **Mercury**	–	tan or sandy (rhodonite, amber)
* **Venus**	–	green (green jasper, aquamarine)
* **Mars**	–	red (garnet, ruby, red jasper, carnelian)
* **Jupiter**	–	blue or blue-flecked (sodalite, turquoise)
* **Saturn**	–	black (jet, tektite, obsidian)

If possible, the stones should be similar in size.
The other six stones should be coloured as follows:

* **Life**	–	blood-red (bloodstone)
* **Luck**	–	rose (rhodochrosite)
* **Magic**	–	pure white (quartz crystal)

* **Love**	–	rose-red or heart-shaped or both (rose quartz)
* **Home**	–	brown (petrified wood)
* **News**	–	multi-coloured (labradorite, amethystine agate)

Ask the questioner to take the Sun, Moon and planetary stones, then concentrate on the question in hand and throw them into a circle, about 40 cm in diameter. The stones that land in the top right-hand portion of the circle are the ones of greater importance and represent the immediate future and influences. Look at the way the stones lie in relation to each other. Look at the ones in the top right-hand portion first and then the middle section. Generally, most of the stones will lie near the middle of the circle and you should look to see if they form a pattern. Traditionally, triangles and circles are good shapes, whereas squares are not so good. Stones that touch each other increase the influences. Any odd stone that lies close to the bottom of the circle is of little significance.

A prominent Saturn stone indicates delays and limitations, while Jupiter represents career and finances. The Sun represents health, happiness and good fortune. Venus represents love, artistic matters, creativity and the feminine aspect, or the female in the life of a man. Mars represents energy, action, difficulties, troubles and the male aspect, or the male in the life of a female. Mercury is communication by letter, telephone, visit or journey. It can also represent doctors, nurses and the healing profession. The Moon represents change and possible delusions and double dealings, depending on which stones are nearby.

Once you have looked at the planetary stones, remove them and ask the questioner to throw the other six stones. If the stones are being thrown onto sand, make sure you smooth the sand over first.

The money and luck stones are the most important and should be dealt with first. For example, should the news and home stones fall together in the top right-hand portion, you could assume that there will be news coming relating to the home. If, on the other hand, the home and money stones fall together, you could interpret this as suggesting money is either coming into or leaving the home. If the luck stone is also nearby, money might be coming into the home, possibly by means of a gift, windfall or legacy of some description.

the zodiac

Gemstones have long been linked with the signs of the zodiac. Indeed, many students of astrology wear the gems associated with their sign, considering them to be lucky. Although it is not widely known, each sign has several possible associated gemstones. This is why stones are often referred to as 'having an affinity with' rather than being specific for a particular zodiac sign.

Those interested in astrology will know that the signs of the zodiac start with Aries and end with Pisces. In this chapter we will look at each sign in turn and discuss the stones that are said to have an affinity with it. We will also discuss the planets associated with each sign, and investigate historical uses of the various stones and their place in traditional folklore. As well as being associated with zodiac signs, stones may be related to the months of the year and we will mention these associations.

Aries people are fiery types, ruled by Mars, so it should come as no surprise that the gemstone most usually associated with them is a red, fiery stone – the garnet. Also associated with Aries are the bloodstone, diamond, carbuncle and ruby.

Garnet

Garnets, most often associated with January birthdates, are a symbol of constancy and friendship and are said to warn the wearer when danger is near. Thought to be especially useful in cases of inflammatory diseases, they are useful for treating rheumatism, arthritis and inflammation of the joints. They are also used for blood problems, as a general tonic, and to aid self-confidence and are said to improve the sex drive! If worn on the left side of the body, garnets are believed to protect against depression as well as rheumatism, and tradition suggests that wearing garnets will bring business success and new opportunities.

Bloodstone

The bloodstone belongs to Rams born in March. Its flecks of red jasper fit in with the Mars and fire themes. Jasper is especially associated with stomach problems and is said to help with digestion if worn against the stomach area. Early Christians, who dedicated a gemstone to each apostle, dedicated jasper to St Peter. It is said that, for early Christians, bloodstone had an association with the Crucifixion. The story goes that on the hill of Calvary, some blood from the crucified Christ fell on the green jasper that lay beneath the cross and speckled it with red. This is probably how the stone got its name.

Ancient civilisations thought bloodstone had the power to cause tempests and that it gave protection against drowning. The reasoning behind this is lost in antiquity. The stone was also used for seals (for example, by the ancient Babylonians), cameos and signets.

Diamond

The diamond, one of the most precious stones, belongs in April. It is said to signify purity and innocence, which is why it is so often seen in engagement rings. Diamonds are supposed to be most powerful when combined with other gemstones and this could have led to the popularity of rings containing diamonds and other stones together.

Diamonds are crystalline forms of carbon and are the hardest stones known. It is said that diamonds belonged to Mars, the god of war (another link with Aries), and that carrying one into battle protected the warrior and guaranteed success, making him invincible and strengthening his muscles. In Roman times, the stone was bound to the left arm of the warrior to bring added strength and courage.

The name 'diamond' comes from a word meaning 'indomitable', and the stone has always been associated with strength. Early Christians associated it with courage. In the Middle Ages it was said to help with madness, nightmares and in curing those who had been poisoned or were subject to some form of pestilence.

Diamond has also been thought to bring good luck. The bloodstone and diamond worn together are said to be particularly lucky. However, very large diamonds are traditionally unlucky and there are many sad tales regarding the owners of unusually large diamonds.

Only in recent centuries have diamonds become such prized possessions. The stones used to be cut in ways that led them to be dull, without the sparkle that characterises them today.

Carbuncle

The carbuncle and ruby are also fiery-red stones, fitting in with the Aries themes. In ancient times, it was felt that both carbuncle and ruby could protect against plague. The name 'carbuncle' comes from a word for coal, and the stone is said to bring hope to unhappy situations. Carbuncles are believed to protect those travelling by land and sea and are very lucky if worn with the aquamarine.

Ruby

The ruby has always been associated with contentment and is considered a symbol of freedom and power, increasing energy levels. It is said to stimulate love if worn close to the heart. It is an aid in stimulating intuitive thought, and is often used as a general tonic. It encourages selflessness and devotion.

The stone is especially valued in India, where it is found in river beds. Sinhalese legend calls rubies 'tears of Buddha' and it is a sacred gem in Buddhism. It is one of many stones that are said to stop bleeding, and is also thought to help people suffering from sadness or melancholy. In the Middle Ages, it was a token of friendship and people believed that in times of trouble it would grow paler. There is a story that Catherine of Aragon wore a ruby in a ring on her little finger and, as her husband's love waned, so the stone became dull and pale. It is also recorded that the ruby set in the state crown of England had an unfortunate history – legend has it that Pedro of Castille so wanted the stone that he murdered the King of Granada to gain possession of it. Worn on the brow, the ruby is thought to give added insight and increased mental powers. The stone is also said to ward off evil spirits, protect against poisons and act as an antidote to a snake bite.

Taurus, 21 April–21 May

The gemstone most usually associated with the Bull is the diamond, which we have already discussed. Bulls with April birthdates may find that the diamond is the stone most suited to them. However, the other affinities, which fit in more properly with the characteristics of Taurus, are coral, emerald, lapis lazuli and jade. Sometimes sapphires too are associated with Taurus, although I would dispute this. Taurus has Venus as its planet.

Emerald

Emerald is a variety of beryl. Beryl has always been associated with the emotions. Emeralds symbolise serenity, success in love, wealth, happiness and peace of mind, and they are said to help with eyesight problems and restore youth (probably the two being linked). Thought to improve the memory and help in cases of insomnia, the emerald also strengthens the immune system. It is a good gemstone to use when meditating, as it assists in deeper spiritual insight. The emerald is considered the stone for May birthdays.

There is evidence that in Roman times wealthy people with eyesight problems wore emerald eye-glasses, and there are stories that the emperor Nero watched gladiatorial combat through an emerald to help his vision. Others thought that the emerald would help in healing ear problems. It has been said that emeralds will help cure ulcers, prevent fits and also ease childbirth! The Romans thought the emerald a remedy for the bite of poisonous spiders, whereas in the Middle East it was said to ensure immortality. Other civilisations considered the emerald a deterrent against being possessed by demons, and in India the stones were often used to decorate temples. In ancient times, due to the ease with which they could be cut, emeralds were the most popular stone and credited with many powers.

If you are in need of confidence, emerald is the stone to wear, as it encourages faith in your own abilities.

Coral

Coral, which is not a true gemstone but a product of marine life, has always been associated with helping to protect against malevolent attack ('the evil eye'). It is usually pink, although sometimes white or red. Its name comes from a Greek word for sea nymph. Coral has associations with stopping blood-flow, helping in cases of anaemia, giving wisdom and preventing madness. Plato suggested that it helped children with toothache and also kept sickness at bay, especially if worn around the neck. Red coral is said to relieve bowel disorders and skin problems and cleanse the system of impurities. Known to help with the throat and voice problems, which beset Taureans, it is also said to strengthen the spleen and is another stone that is thought to lose its colour when the owner is ill.

Jade

Jade has always been popular with the Chinese. It appears in many of their temples and has been used in powdered form as an internal treatment. In ancient times, jade was more highly prized than gold and was linked with eternity. The Maoris of New Zealand often use it in their weapons.

Traditionally associated with the month of May, jade is said to relieve renal problems, protect wounds from becoming inflamed, and help with eye diseases. It is often linked with women, helping with all kinds of female disorders.

Yellow jade is thought to aid digestive problems. The stone is also said to assist wisdom and bring tranquillity, being credited with longevity and fertility. Jade is said to guard against lightning.

Lapis lazuli

Lapis lazuli, or more properly 'lazurite', is a beautiful blue-green rock. Referred to in ancient times as the 'stone of Heaven', and more recently as the 'night stone', it is usually found in limestone near granitic rocks, enclosing grains of pyrite, especially in Italy, Chile and Turkey. It also has strong associations with the Egyptians, who often wore the stone as a talisman to ward off danger. It has been used to treat eye problems, powdered down to a paste, steeped in water and used as a poultice. It was also thought to be an aid in cases of epilepsy and a protection against hazards. More recently it has been used to help with thyroid problems and neuralgia.

Lapis lazuli is a powerful gemstone and should be worn therefore only by those who have sufficient strength of character and body to deal with its powers. People of a sensitive nature may find it overpowering unless it is encased in glass or crystal. It is said to be particularly useful in treating thyroid conditions and for enhancing psychic abilities, helping us to get in touch with our higher selves. It is a good stone to wear when making decisions.

The stones associated with Gemini are agate (especially moss agate or banded agate, the latter showing lines of light and dark, red and white), beryl, chrysolite, onyx and peridot. The planet associated with Gemini is Mercury.

Agate

Agates are types of chalcedony or cryptocrystalline quartz and are usually brown, dark red or yellow. Named after the river Achates in Sicily, they are now found in India, Brazil and Germany. For centuries they have been thought to bring luck to people working with or on the land.

The agate was held in great esteem by ancient civilisations, who thought it was representative of the third eye and spiritual love. Probably the connection with the third eye leads it to be used for eye problems and headaches. Ground to a powder, the stone was often used to stop bleeding and soothe irritations and skin diseases.

There are many types of agate but all are said to bring about good fortune, good health, eloquence, wealth and long life. Reputedly used by athletes since ancient times to increase vitality, the agate increases not only energy levels but also self-confidence, as it banishes fear. It was believed to help with epilepsy. An agate was traditionally thought to bestow the gifts of eloquence, social grace and good fortune on its owner. These earthy stones help to keep the Gemini grounded, and promote truth. To strengthen agate's powers, the chrysoprase should also be worn.

Beryl

Beryl is usually green, but sometimes has yellow, pink, blue and white shades within it. Known to have been one of the first crystals used by ancient seers, beryl is said to help those lacking motivation to move forward by improving willpower.

In the Middle Ages, beryl was thought to cure laziness and banish fear and was linked with emotional difficulties. It was also said to help with asthma and kidney stones, as well as liver disease. In more recent times, the beryl has been used to treat throat problems and is a particularly good stone for meditation.

Chrysolite

Chrysolite is most commonly olive green, but can also be brown or red. It gets its name from the Greek *chiastos*, meaning 'marked with an x'. For this reason, it is sometimes called 'the cross stone', and was also known as 'the golden stone' to the ancients.

For chrysolite to exert its full power, it is said that it should be set in gold. Known to be very useful in cases of viral illness, it is also used against toxemia. In ancient times, chrysolite was thought to be a cure for insomnia and to protect against nightmares, when worn at night, and to dispel melancholy and improve creativity when worn during the day. In medieval times, it was believed to prevent madness.

Onyx

Onyx, a type of coloured chalcedony, has long been associated with improving concentration and devotion and it is not surprising, therefore, that many rosaries are made from this stone. It is also said to help with stress and aid inner serenity. It is used to improve concentration, self-control and hearing difficulties.

Peridot

Peridot is often recommended for sleeplessness, digestive problems, reducing stress and helping with lethargy by stimulating the mind. It is also said to help with lung congestion and stomach ulcers.

Cancer, 22 June–23 July

Cancer's connections with the Moon are followed through in its gemstone associations, moonstone, chrysoprase, pearl and selenite. July's stone is traditionally ruby, which we have already discussed.

Moonstone

Moonstone is a variety of feldspar. It has a pearly appearance and can be grey, white, pale yellow or almost colourless. Said to grow stronger and weaker as the moon waxes and wanes, it is a symbol of hope and is especially protective to seafarers. The moonstone is so abundant in Ceylon that it is sometimes called the 'Ceylon opal'. In India, the moonstone was sacred for lovers.

It is said to help reduce fevers, promote long life and happiness and attract friendship. A feminine stone, used to help with menstruation and child-bearing, it maintains emotional balance and is sometimes called 'Mother Earth's stone'. It is used by men who wish to get in touch with the female side of their personalities and as an aid to understanding dreams.

In ancient times, this stone was said to protect travellers, especially those travelling by sea and was considered a protection against dropsy, fluid retention and urinary problems.

Chrysoprase

Chrysoprase is a bright green type of chalcedony and is sometimes called the 'joy stone', as it helps ease depression and anxiety, bringing joy, cheerfulness and personal insight. It should not be kept in direct sunlight, as this may cause its colour to fade. As it is said to improve memory and reduce nervousness, people often take it into exams with them. It also helps the mind to adapt to emergency situations.

In ancient times, it was believed that the stone would lose its colour if kept in the presence of poisons. Often worn as a remedy for gout and rheumatism, the stone was also used to treat kidney and bladder problems. Tradition suggests that it will strengthen the sight of anyone who looks into it for any length of time.

This is said to be a particularly lucky stone if worn with agate.

Selenite

Selenite or gypsum is reputed to be a rejuvenator, helping with many problems, from improving skin texture to increasing fertility.

Easily chipped and very soft, it is often used to relieve stress and help with nervous problems.

Pearl

For centuries pearls have been considered an emblem of purity, innocence and peace. Pearls were great favourites in medieval times, and were thought to symbolise purity and chastity. Alchemists often dissolved pearls in lemon juice and gave the resultant liquid to patients suffering from internal bleeding, as well as other internal problems. There are stories of pearls being ground to a fine powder and drunk in milk to cure irritability, weak eyes, consumption and the plague!

Associated with June, pearls are particularly fortunate for Cancerians with a birthdate in that month.

Because they are regarded as symbols of the moon, pearls are often thought to be unlucky. Many people refuse to accept pearls as gifts, suggesting that they bring about an unhappy marriage. The reason behind this may be that pearls can resemble tears and indeed, they have been described as 'solidified tears'. I personally do not believe any gemstone to be unlucky. If you care for your pearls and look after them, they can surely do you no harm.

Divers still wear pearls in shark-infested waters, due to the tradition that they protect the wearer from such creatures.

Pearls are considered lucky when worn with emeralds and moonstones.

Leo, 24 July–23 August

The Lion, ruled by the Sun, has amber, aventurine, topaz, onyx and diamond as its stones. Onyx and diamond have other affinities, already discussed. July has ruby as its association, whereas August has sardonyx, the stone of sociability.

Sardonyx

Sardonyx is a white and dark brown or red variety of onyx. Once believed to be a pain reliever, it is said to symbolise happiness in marriage and in friendship.

It was reputed to have the power to protect against the plague, stings and bites and to give popularity to the wearer. It was widely used in Roman times and often found in brooches of the period, due to the ease with which it can be engraved. Tradition suggested that unmarried women who wore the stone would never be wed, but those who were married and about to give birth were expected to find great comfort from this stone!

Amber

Amber is formed from the fossilised solidified resin of trees. It is often found in large lumps weighing many pounds and can be ground into a powder to give for various internal complaints or burnt to provide an aromatic vapour. It is said to help with heart problems and to help ward off the plague and curses, by absorbing negativities. It is a harmonising stone, useful in the relief of stress and asthma and as a de-toxifier. It is sometimes called the 'mindful stone' because it is said to contain vibrations from the past and increase memory.

In ancient times, amber was often worn around the throat, as a protection against catarrh, asthma and hay fever. Powdered and mixed with oil, it was used as a body preparation to ease aching muscles. Thought to help with bronchial problems, it was used for the mouthpieces of tobacco pipes in times gone by.

Other stones closely related to amber include krantzite and beckerite.

Aventurine

There are two different minerals called 'aventurine' – the one I refer to here is the green quartz, rather than the feldspar also known as 'sunstone'. Aventurine is said to purify and strengthen the body, mind and spirit. Those suffering from anxiety might find it offers some relief by helping them to focus on their problems. The stone is associated with bringing good health and well-being and reputed to be of help with exams. It may also be useful for people suffering from migraines, as discussed earlier.

Topaz

Also associated with November and with Jupiter, topaz is a stone with a wide tradition of applications – from helping in childbirth to warding off the plague. It is found in pink, yellow, green, blue or white forms.

Topaz can be changed by heat, pressure and friction. The stone exhibits strong electric currents. Said to be able to detoxify the body and regenerate organs and glands, it helps to soothe and give inner peace to those with problems. Affected by the phases of the moon, topaz reputedly helps with eye disorders, cures baldness, prevents asthma and helps with sleep disorders when used as a gem elixir. It is said to promise its owner a long and happy life, and is associated with faithfulness. Eastern mystics believe this stone helps ease the pain of death and enables those who use it during meditation to see into the future.

Tradition suggests that if topaz is worn on the left-hand side of the body, it can help overcome grief; worn over the stomach, it will protect from stomach disorders by calming negative emotions. Since ancient times it has been used to help with female disorders, lung complaints, epilepsy, bladder troubles and problems with the nose and throat.

The amethystine sapphire will increase the power of the topaz.

Virgo, 24 August–23 September

Agate, jasper, tourmaline, chalcedony and carnelian are all associated with Virgo, whereas September has associations with the sapphire. Virgo is another sign ruled by Mercury.

Sapphire

Sapphires have been regarded for centuries as highly spiritual stones. A ring containing diamonds and sapphires is said to be exceptionally lucky, sapphires having been associated always with luck in romance. Sapphire is said to bring peace and happiness, and will help with the heart and stomach and also with stimulating the pituitary glands and psychic centres. Its primary role, however, lies in the field of mental health.

In ancient times sapphire was used to treat eye disorders and as an amulet to give protection from bewitchment and to guard the chastity of its owner. It would dim if there were signs of fraud or treachery.

The sapphire's power will be increased if it is worn with the turquoise stone.

Tourmaline

Tourmaline generally ranges from dark green to black, although other colours are fairly common. It is a healing stone, which will enhance the healing potential of other stones with which it is kept in contact. Used by astrologers in the past at times of planetary change, to ease the transitions (it wards off negative energy), it should be worn next to the skin for best effect. It is said to help with nervous troubles and stress-related problems and to give confidence and protection by reducing negativities. Therefore this is another stone that is often taken into exam rooms.

Often carried in ancient times as an amulet, it is believed to give its wearer added perception.

Chalcedony

Chalcedony, named after the Greek city of Chalcedon, is a bluish-grey stone which is seldom used but said to be helpful in cases of bad temper or unease, bringing about feelings of peace and serenity. As such, this gemstone should have many applications in our modern world!

Believed by the ancients to give physical strength and heal gallstones, it was also used to deliver people from nightmares.

Carnelian

Carnelian is usually red but can also be brown and off-white. It is sometimes called the 'blood stone' and was used in times gone by to stop the flow of blood, especially nosebleeds. Carnelian is a strong gemstone, a reputedly powerful healer, helping to balance and energise the body and particularly useful for gallbladder and liver problems.

Popular in Arab countries and found in inlays on jewellery and sarcophagi, the stone is thought to promote long life and eliminate fear by keeping the wearer 'grounded' and rational. It is considered helpful with nervous problems when worn next to the skin, and good fortune is said to follow those who carry the stone.

In more modern times carnelian has been used to increase creativity in speech and mind. Many public speakers carry this stone with them.

Libra, 24 September–23 October

There are strong associations with the opal (considered by many to be unlucky). Rose quartz, emerald and malachite are also stones with an affinity for the Libran, and Venus is the planet for this sign.

Opal

The opal was once considered a symbol of hope, bringing the wearer love and lasting happiness. The stone defies description, containing fire sparks, delicate shades and a full spectrum of colour. Formed from shells and the skeletons of tiny animals, opals are very porous and at least 30 per cent water. As a consequence, they should never be immersed in water or brought into contact with oils – those with opal rings take note!

For the ancients, especially the Greeks and Romans, the opal was thought to give direction if held between the eyes. It was known as the 'stone of vision' or 'gem of hope'. They also believed it would look after both children and the arts, and described it as 'the gem of the gods'.

A strong healing stone, said to enhance intuition, help with eyesight (it is sometimes called the 'ophthalmois' or 'eye stone') and bring relaxation, to the point of total peace, opal can be used to put the wearer in touch with his or her higher self. It is reputed to lose its lustre if touched by an unfaithful lover, and was considered unlucky because of its variable colour. Used by those with lung complaints, it is also said to help with the assimilation of proteins into the system.

The opal will increase in power if worn with the lapis lazuli and is especially helpful to those born in October.

Malachite

Malachite is another healing stone, its green stripes able to soothe and bring about restful sleep, as well as to help with circulation difficulties and balance the emotions. This stone containing copper (as do turquoise and chrysocolla) is also useful in treating rheumatism and toothache. Malachite is also called the 'peacock stone', a name given by the ancient Romans, who believed it would help with colds, bleeding, vertigo and babies' teething problems. It is said to attract love to its wearer and in the USA is thought to bring wealth – or love of money! Malachite is an exceptionally good stone to use in meditation.

Rose quartz

Rose quartz is said to be capable of changing negative into positive energies. It is often called the 'stone of unconditional love', pink being associated with this quality. When kept in a living room, the stone is thought to help diffuse stressful situations and heal emotional wounds.

Excellent to use for migraines and headaches, rose quartz promotes peace and healing, stimulates the imagination and intellect and reduces feelings of anger, resentment and guilt. It is said to increase fertility (possibly because of its association with love) and is one of the strongest healing stones available.

Scorpio, 24 October–22 November

Magnetite, obsidian, smoky quartz, jasper and aquamarine are all associated with the Scorpion, while November is associated with topaz. Mars and Pluto are the associated planets.

Aquamarine

Aquamarine is usually blue-green but can also be yellow, and is another 'exam stone'. Said to banish nerves and fear and protect the wearer from poisons, it is most often used for ridding a person of unhappiness. This is a stone of happiness in marriage and well-being, bringing its wearer clarity of mind and purpose. Aquamarine is also reputed to help with glandular problems, disorders of the throat, stomach and eyes, and fluid retention. Often used in meditation, this stone from the beryl family is thought to protect the wearer from accidents, especially when travelling by sea.

To increase the power of this stone, it should be worn with the carbuncle.

Obsidian

Obsidian is volcanic lava and is often used to improve poor eyesight. Considered a 'male' stone, probably because when cut and polished it makes effective spearheads and knife blades, it is said to help those embarking upon a spiritual quest, keeping energies stable and clearing blockages. It is said that those who wear this stone will never shed tears of grief. This reputedly powerful healer is another stone that needs to be used wisely, and only by those capable of dealing with its power.

Smoky quartz

Smoky quartz has for generations been considered a good luck charm or talisman. It was often given to soldiers about to go into battle. An aid in relieving negativity and promoting relaxation, this stone is often used in meditation, and if kept under a pillow at night, it is said to induce lucid dreams. The ancients considered the smoky quartz helpful in cases of infertility.

A word of warning: genuine smoky quartz is produced by natural radioactive materials, but it can also be man-made, in which case it is usually very dark or black. True smoky quartz should be brown. It is always preferable to use the natural stone, as man-made stones do not have the same qualities, and the healing properties will be impaired.

Magnetite

Magnetite is not often used, but is particularly useful in cases of rheumatism. Said to be an energy restorer, this black stone is sometimes also called 'lodestone' and is useful for meditation, as an aid in acquiring wisdom and intuition. It may also be able to help with liver problems and even in premature baldness.

Sagittarius, 23 November–21 December

Amethyst, spinel sapphire and turquoise are all associated with Sagittarius, whereas topaz is often connected with the month of November. Jupiter is connected with Sagittarians.

Amethyst

Amethyst, together with rose quartz, is probably one of the most popular gemstones now. Ancients thought it a cure for drunkenness, probably because its name comes from a Greek word implying sobriety, and those who wore it believed that they could drink as much as they wished without any ill effects. The Romans often used amethyst cups to help the drinker to remain sober. Because of the darkness of the cups, the contents could be well watered, without anyone noticing, and perhaps this was why they stayed sober! Amethyst is reputed to lose its brightness in the presence of poison and to pale if the wearer is ill.

Also associated with February, the amethyst gives serenity and steadfastness and has long been associated with St Valentine, bringing happiness in love and good luck. It is often used in religious circles, both in rings and rosaries. Also, an amethyst wrapped in thin silk and held over the temples is said to soothe nervous headaches. Tradition suggests, however, that the stone should first be warmed, either by the sun's rays or by the warmth of a natural fire.

Considered a spiritual stone, the amethyst has long had the reputation of being able to increase the owner's ability to develop spiritually, purify and heal, and is very commonly used by healers to induce calm and alleviate stress and loneliness. Used in meditation, for guidance and help, the amethyst will help bring clear thoughts and calm the mind, as well as help with headaches. I have used it for this purpose and can vouch for these claims. A very powerful stone, the amethyst provides a link between the higher and lower states of consciousness.

During the Middle Ages the amethyst was quite rare and was highly prized and it is still used in the rings of Roman Catholic bishops. It has been connected with Sagittarius since the beginnings of modern astrology.

Spinel

Spinel, sometimes also called 'spinal ruby', is usually a lovely red colour. It is said to give added strength of purpose to its owner and bring clarity of mind, especially in business matters. Thought by the ancients to prevent damage from storms, it is now said to help in cases of nausea and sickness.

Turquoise

Associated with December birthdays and so most properly used by Archers born in that month, turquoise was used as a charm by Indian medicine men, who valued it as a powerful healer. Some American Indians still consider the stone to be sacred.

It is reputed to be a love charm, and is another stone that is believed to change colour if the lover is unfaithful or, indeed, if its wearer is close to death. In addition, turquoise is considered a stone of friendship and loyalty. Should your turquoise start to pale, don't worry – simply leave it off for a few weeks and it should return to its normal brilliance.

In ancient times turquoise was used to ward off accidents and given as a comfort to those about to undergo surgery. People who travel on horseback may wish to wear this stone, as it is said to ensure the horse's surefootedness.

Thought to bring prosperity and luck, especially if worn with a sapphire, the turquoise is reputed to promote the regeneration of cells, protect against pollutants and strengthen the body. It is believed to help with bad eyesight and, if applied in a poultice to the chest area, to help with bronchial problems.

Traditionally, the turquoise stone should be a gift and it is considered to be unlucky to buy your own. It is particularly powerful if worn with the blue sapphire.

Capricorn, 22 December–20 January

Jet and tiger's eye are associated with the Goat, and January, as already mentioned, is associated with the garnet. Capricorn is ruled by Saturn.

Jet

Considered by the ancient Britons to be a magical stone, jet is a fossilised plant and not a stone at all. In early British history it was frequently used, burnt, to repel curses and the plague. It was taken powdered in wine and water as a cure for toothache or when teeth became loose. Used also to help with skin problems, prevent hysteria and for many female disorders, it was said to counteract magic spells and protect the wearer from bites. Queen Victoria wore jet after the death of Prince Albert, and it became synonymous with women in mourning in the latter part of the nineteenth century. It was also used in amulets to prevent hallucinations.

In more recent times, the jet has been used to treat migraine. It is another substance that can be faked – plastic, rubber and glass have all passed as jet.

Jet is particularly powerful if worn with the ruby.

Tiger's eye

Tiger's eye, another quartz, is a very useful stone for many Capricorns and also for people who worry about their health, as it is said to guard against hypochondria and psychosomatic illness. Giving confidence and inner strength, it is said to encourage creative pursuits, calm and balance.

Traditionally used for healing problems with the lower legs and feet, tiger's eye was also considered useful for healing the eyes, probably due to its name rather than any special qualities. It is known to be useful for digestive problems (especially those with a nervous origin) and can be particularly useful to Capricorns who are stubborn and intransigent, as it is said to 'ground' and balance.

Aquarius, 21 January–19 February

Four of the stones associated with Aquarians – amethyst, chalcedony, aquamarine and turquoise – have already been discussed, since they are associated with other signs too. In addition, Aquarius is connected with lepidolite, zircon and celestite. Aquarians are ruled by Saturn and Uranus.

Lepidolite

This unusual stone has a high lithium content and is very helpful in balancing out the compulsive behaviour for which Aquarians are notorious. It is also useful as an aid to psychic development, helping to inspire, illuminate and develop the link between the conscious lower mind and the higher mind.

If lepidolite is used with kunzite, another unusual stone, the results are said to be quite spectacular, especially in developing healing talents.

Celestite

Celestite is a relaxing stone, helping its owner to unwind from even the most stressful circumstances, and aiding and accelerating spiritual growth and creative expression. Said to impart clear speech and clarity of thought, this stone should, in truth, be far more popular in this modern age.

Zircon

Zircon is a multi-coloured stone that helps to calm emotions and protect against depression. Its ability to help increase self-esteem and spiritual insight make it another true New Age stone. Used by the ancients to help treat fevers, the zircon is also useful in cases of insomnia and is said to increase the appetite.

Crystal, as well as chrysolite and bloodstone (already discussed), is connected with Pisces. The ruling planet for Pisces is Neptune.

Crystal

Crystal – quartz crystal or rock crystal – is probably the most powerful stone known. It is used in modern technology. It is also used by many as an aid to meditation, which releases the owner's higher consciousness and can accelerate spiritual growth, spiritual development and healing.

Tradition suggests that a cup made of quartz crystal will turn cloudy if poison is added to the drink it contains and so in ancient times many goblets were made of crystal. The ancients used this stone to amplify the rays of the sun and bring heat to the body, as well as in a powdered form for many types of ailment.

Probably the most powerful general healer, the quartz crystal attracts energy and light and is often employed as an aid in psychic development, facilitating meditation, dispelling negativity and inspiring communication with the higher self. Quartz crystal is often used as a charging crystal for other stones and is widely used in the East for magical purposes in the form of charms and talismans. It is said to promote a deep sleep if worn at night and to protect against evil.

It is particularly powerful if worn or used with amethyst.

A stone that attracts you

We have covered all the signs of the zodiac and the stones associated with them. Whatever your birth sign, ruling planet or best-aspected planets, I truly feel that you can be attracted to a particular stone. If this happens to you and the stone is not one of those listed for your sign, please don't turn away from it. There may be several reasons why you are drawn to purchase a stone at a particular time and, therefore, the right stone for you may have no connection at all with your birth sign or planets. You are an individual; trust your own instincts and always be true to yourself.

Conclusion

Modern technology may seem to drive us further and further away from natural remedies, actions and thoughts. Crystals and gemstones have been with us a very long time – in fact, they predate the evolution of human beings. They are part of planet Earth in the same way as we are, and form part of the order of the universe.

If used properly, wisely and well, gemstones and crystals can help in many forms of healing, meditation, self-development, self-awareness and personal growth. As we have seen, there are many and varied crystals to choose from and only practice will ensure their correct use.

Much modern thought on crystals and gemstones is confusing. Please don't expect to be a professional crystal therapist having read this one book. This takes years of study and practice, and even then, as most therapists will tell you, you continue to learn.

Lightning Source UK Ltd.
Milton Keynes UK
UKHW02f1330050418
320562UK00005B/479/P